Looking for
Comfortable Shoes

Looking for Comfortable Shoes

JACKIE GANEM

iUniverse, Inc.
Bloomington

LOOKING FOR COMFORTABLE SHOES

iUniverse books may be ordered through booksellers or by contacting:

iUniverse
1663 Liberty Drive
Bloomington, IN 47403
www.iuniverse.com
1-800-Authors (1-800-288-4677)

Because of the dynamic nature of the Internet, any web addresses or links contained in this book may have changed since publication and may no longer be valid. The views expressed in this work are solely those of the author and do not necessarily reflect the views of the publisher, and the publisher hereby disclaims any responsibility for them.

Any people depicted in stock imagery provided by Thinkstock are models, and such images are being used for illustrative purposes only.
Certain stock imagery © Thinkstock.

ISBN: 978-1-4620-4224-1 (sc)
ISBN: 978-1-4620-4225-8 (hc)
ISBN: 978-1-4620-4226-5 (ebk)

Library of Congress Control Number: 2011913383

Printed in the United States of America

iUniverse rev. date: 12/30/2011

For Andrew, Anne, Sarah, and JoAnn

The great loves of my life

Author's Note

I have written my book in two parts each as a collection of small stories. The first part is about growing up in a Lebanese immigrant family; the second part is the story of a passionless marriage and a family tragedy that forever changes the course of our lives.

This is a true story. However, it is my story and is filtered through my sensibilities. This is as I know it to be.

Acknowledgements

"Thank you" is not enough to say to Robert B. and Joan H. Parker. The gentle encouragement from Joan and the direct honesty from Bob were just right to get me going and keep me focused to finish the work. It has taken love and support, too, and JoAnn has given me that.

I'd like also to thank Jane Katims and her writers group for reading and listening carefully to what I have to say.

All have given me the courage to write my story. I am immensely grateful.

We . . . write to heighten our own awareness of life. We write to taste life twice, in the moment and in retrospection. We write to be able to transcend our life, to reach beyond it . . . to teach ourselves to speak with others, to record the journey into the labyrinth."

—Anais Nin, The Diary of Anais Nin: Volume Five

The Beginning

Growing up, I felt little sparks all around me. Some of the sparks landed on me and some did not. Some of the sparks that landed on me stayed to form a bigger spark. And some of the big sparks cut through me to the core and are with me to this day. I call them sparks because they are bright and sharp, and they have not dimmed at all with time. They are different colors. Some are bright like the sun, some are blue and purple and sad, and some are red like fire and blister like a burn. The mix is what matters.

The sparks are stories, and I grew up with hundreds of them. Some stories became legends. Some were repeated like a Greek chorus featuring my great aunts. They had their own brand of story, their own brand of history as they lived it when they first arrived in America from Lebanon in 1903.

They felt duped when they arrived, having been seduced by posters in Beirut, which promised great prosperity in America working in the woolen mills in Lawrence, Massachusetts. The opportunity turned out to be working six days a week, ten hours a day for the sum of five or six dollars. The climax of this story was the Bread and Roses Strike of 1912. My Great Aunt Lamia was in that strike, arrested with hundreds of other immigrants. She lived ninety-five years and never failed to tell the story whenever someone asked. It was a defining moment for her and for others in the family. She always ended the story with, "You see, that's why I am a communist." No one in the family thought she knew what a communist was, but we were clear on the meaning of the story.

Most of the stories we grew up with speak to the insecurities and uncertainties all new immigrant groups felt in a new country, speaking a new language, and coping with a new way of living. The mill owners thrived on the immigrants' insecurities. It worked best for them if no one spoke English. English would unite the groups and perhaps cause problems for the management of the mills. Control and obedience were key to the mills' success. After the strike and Aunt Lamia's arrest, the rest of the family decided that it would be best to earn a living providing goods and services to the Lebanese community. Working in the mills was too dangerous, and the money was not enough to support their big families. Sitho took in boarders. My grandfathers both went into the food business. Gido Corey went into the wholesale fruit and vegetable business, and Gido Ganem went into the retail food business.

Work was all they knew. Both families were shrewd. They trusted almost no one and did business cautiously. The small circle of people they trusted included family first and then those in the same community or church. They learned to speak English and could count in all the languages of the immigrant communities: Italian, French, and German.

They had enough success to buy houses for their families. Of course, they had to buy through a straw man. The "good" neighborhoods didn't want olive-skinned

Lebanese as neighbors.

There was a focus and bravery about them, a single mindedness that was clear and simple. For those that followed, the world became much more complex. That first generation needed to answer the question, "How does one become an American?"

The aunts were keepers of the traditions and the language. They were keepers of the recipes for Lebanese foods. They were keepers of the water pipe and card games. They were keepers of the manners of hospitality. They were of one mind with all of these things. No one escaped scrutiny.

"The Americans don't know how to cook."

"The Americans don't know what good food is."

"The Italians are short."

"You can't trust the French."

"The Jews are shrewd but the Arabs are shrewder."

"It's okay to fight with people outside the family; it is not okay to fight with anyone inside the family."

"You can't do business with the Yankees. They would rather have the turkeys die of old age than take a penny off the price!"

"It's better to fit in than not fit in."

The list was very long, and it was not easy to march through all of the rules without bumping into a few. It's like having sparks fly all around and trying to dodge them to not get burned.

So why is any of this important? The stories we grow up with are our links to the past and help us to understand our own stories.

There are times when it is not a good thing to be different, and there are times we strive to be different. My grandparents wanted to fit in to their new country and to follow the rules as they saw them in their new life. They began their life in Lawrence, Massachusetts in the Lebanese section of the city around the Lebanese Catholic Church on Elm Street.

My father's family came from Salbeen, a small mountain village, and they arrived with limited resources. Gido Ganem (my grandfather, Joseph Ganem), heard about the opportunities in America and left to explore them leaving Sitho (my grandmother) in Salbeen with four children. Sitho was twenty-three years old, having married when she was fifteen like most women in the village of Salbeen. Gido Joseph had a cousin in Lawrence and that is how he came to settle there. He sent for his family. The year was 1905. My father was the third child and was three years old when he arrived in America.

That same year, my mother's father, George Corey, and his two brothers came to Lawrence in search of a new life. Their name was Khoury but it was changed at Ellis Island by an Irish immigration worker. The Coreys originally lived in Beirut and were political activists. They left the country because they were rebels against the Moslem government in power at the time, and there was a bounty on their heads. They had to leave or suffer imprisonment or worse.

My maternal grandmother, Sitho Akaber Kawash, was new to America, too. She and her family were from Hasbiah, just outside Beirut. They traveled by camel to Beirut and came to America in 1904. She was a teenage girl, and she and her sisters had jobs in the woolen mills. They all lived between Elm and White Streets, the center of the Lebanese community, near the coffee house and the Lebanese Catholic Church, Saint Anthony's. Akaber and George met and married in Lawrence in 1905.

George and Joseph met and became friends soon after they arrived. They were an unlikely twosome. Gido Joseph was quiet, shy and simple. Gido George was gregarious, outgoing, and drank a lot of arak (the Lebanese version of anisette). He loved to talk and laugh. Gido Joseph had no sense of humor.

The coffee house on Elm Street was the men's gathering place, where news was shared and plans made. Joseph Ganem and George Corey met and became partners in a wholesale fruit and produce business, first selling to the Lebanese community and then branching out to all of Lawrence and its quilt of immigrants. The two men could not have been more different, but the relationship worked for a while. Joseph was a simple man who knew nothing of worldly things like politics. He only knew hard work. He didn't smoke, he didn't drink, he talked very little, and he never laughed. George was always talking, laughing, and drinking. He loved people and people loved him. He was fun and fast-moving. He made friends with everyone, not just the Lebanese. Joseph never learned to speak much English. George spoke English and several other languages.

The partnership worked well for a few years. George had all the contacts and Joseph carried through with the work. Uncle Bill, Joseph's oldest son, also worked with them. George went to Boston to do the buying. He had a magic about him when dealing with people. He would bring the fruits and vegetables back with horse and buggy, and Joseph would deliver and collect money. George's boisterous bravado did not wear well with Joseph. Joseph was also concerned with George's influence on his growing family. There was a wildness about George that Joseph could not accept. They parted ways amicably and each went into business alone, keeping a quiet respect for each other.

When my parents married in July 1931, they moved into the "Big House" at 46 Pleasant Street in Methuen, Massachusetts. We called it the Big House, because the whole Ganem family lived there together.

My brother Billy was born in August 1932. He was a beautiful baby with hazel eyes, almost-blond hair with curls, and a very sweet disposition. It didn't hurt that he was a boy. The family thought Billy was beautiful. My mother dressed him up every day and walked with him on Pleasant Street. When she didn't have time, a neighborhood teenager walked him around. My mother's mother, Akaber, was still living at that time, and she would visit with her sisters, the Aunts. They passed Billy from lap to lap and exclaimed with every move, *"Hallween h'il wiche"* (How beautiful, his face.). Sitho Ganem, my father's mother, loved the visits. She was proud of her family and newest grandson. The visit also gave her a chance to speak Arabic and feel at home with the Aunts. Billy was named after Uncle Bill, my father's oldest brother. This gave Billy a key place in the bosom of the Ganem family.

I was born in March 1934. My Sitho Akaber, died unexpectedly in January of that year from an infection contracted during routine surgery. She was only forty-eight years old. Pictures of my mother at that time show the grief on her face. She wore black for two years after her mother's death. I was a difficult breach birth that my mother felt certain was the result of the trauma of her mother's death. She told that story countless times over the years. I got the message, and it was a tough beginning.

There I was, a very difficult birth, a girl, and not born into the happiest house, either. Next to Billy, I guess I was no beauty. More than once I heard, "You had ears that stuck out and black hair that looked like feathers." My mother kept me in the bedroom most of the time. She tried to fix me up by putting tape on my ears to hold them back, closer to my head. It didn't work. "The only thing it did was make you cry when I pulled the tape off and pulled out some of your hair with it," she said. In every picture I have seen of myself as a baby and toddler, I had a huge ribbon in my hair. It must have been there to distract from the ears and feathers.

The Aunts visited often to see Billy and me, the new baby. There would have been a lot to say about the baby, her hair and her ears, all in Arabic. I do know there is an Arabic saying that loosely translates to the one we know as, "Homely in the cradle, pretty at the table." That would have been the consolation expressed to my mother.

My mother was always nervous in the Big House, nervous that she was not pleasing everyone or that her children were not doing the right things or not being polite to all the grown ups. If only she could have spoken for each of us all the time, she would have been happy. She did the next best thing.

Whenever we were in a large group of family members, my mother would watch us very closely, especially me. It didn't seem to matter as much how my brothers spoke. If anyone asked me a question, my mother would mouth the words as I spoke them, sort of like a ventriloquist, except I could see her mouth moving. If a smile was required, I would get that message, too; she would smile as she mouthed the words for me. If I could see her mouth move, then I guessed everyone could see it. I tried not to sit or stand too near my mother because, if I did, it usually meant a pinch or a push to either talk or not talk or say, "No thank you," or "Thank you," or "Hello," or something else. The messages were constant, and I was never clear who I should be looking at when I spoke. Should I look at my mother for more cues, or should I look at the person to whom I was speaking? Unless it was absolutely necessary, we stayed away from the crowd. It was much simpler that way. I never noticed any other mother doing the "lip-mouth" thing. I guess they didn't care as much as my mother.

My mother was convinced that one of my hips was higher than the other. This was just before we moved out of the Big House. She had taken me to an orthopedic doctor, Dr. Macausland, for an examination. I had to stand in front of both of them in my cotton lollypop underwear while they discussed what they each saw. He took my measurements, checked my weight, height, and posture, and more. Dr. Macausland was a friend of the family and probably didn't want to say there was nothing wrong or tell my mother to relax and forget about my hip. He suggested she bring me back in a year for another look.

That wasn't quite enough for my mother. The next Sunday when my Uncle Emil, my father's youngest brother, was home from medical school, she asked him to take a look. She might as well have asked me to take all my clothes off and stand in front of everyone. I numbed myself as much as I could, and did what I was told. I was getting good at turning off the world. He didn't see what my mother saw and told my mother to forget about my hip. It was the only time I remember liking Uncle Emil.

Chapter 1

Sitho (Grandma) Ganem

The big house always felt warm and smelled like freshly baked bread. I knew that when I opened the door, Sitho would be there waiting for me. She didn't speak English, so we communicated with gestures and the few words we both understood.

Everyone called it the Big House simply because of its size and the fact that we all lived there together. The house was set on a hill with a stone wall shielding it from the street. There were four acres of land around the house with apple, pear, and peach trees. There were also some out-buildings filled with tools and unused equipment from businesses either just closed or about to be opened by someone in the family.

The Big House always felt warm and smelled like freshly baked bread. I knew that when I opened the door, Sitho Ganem would be there waiting for me. She was the heart and soul of the Big House. People swirled around inside and out—talking, moving, cleaning, eating, and talking some more. Sitho Ganem never said too much, even in Arabic, but she quietly made herself known. Her five sons and husband were busy in their own world outside the Big House. They talked about the world outside, the town, the state, and the world. Sometimes she listened. If she did speak during those gatherings, they would all stop and listen to what she had to say.

My Father was a large and direct man, but when he spoke to his mother, he was gentle and sweet, kissing her hello and good-bye. There was a crowd of people in the house—grandparents, parents, cousins, aunts, and uncles—but I often felt lonely and confused. The one thing that was clear to me was the love I felt from Sitho Ganem and my father.

My father left for work before I was up and if I saw him at night it was usually for just a minute before I went to bed. I saw Sitho Ganem every day. She was in the kitchen early, cooking before anyone else was awake. She touched me every day. She touched my head, buttoned my coat, or tied my shoes. I loved that. When I came home from school, she often called to me, "*Thi lahoun ya binthe*" ("Come here, my child"). I would sit on the floor in front of her while she gently moved her thumb and forefingers through my hair. It was a gentle movement that felt wonderful and loving. I have always loved having my head touched. It wasn't until many years later that I learned she was looking for lice.

The Big House was at once wonderful and frightening. It was wonderful because it was so big and full of great mysterious places to play in and to explore. It was frightening for the same reasons. There were eight bedrooms. My mother, father, two brothers, and I shared two bedrooms. Usually, no one else in the house came into those rooms. The general living area had a huge kitchen with a table that fourteen of us could sit around at once. There were three living rooms on the first floor. Each one had its own function—one was for family members, one was used only when company came to visit, and the other one was never used. It was called the Oriental Room. It had furniture from the old country that was precious to all the grownups and that the children were never allowed to touch.

The men were up and out early, but some of them came home for lunch. Sitho Ganem was in charge of all things in the kitchen. Her husband, Gido (grandfather) Ganem spent his days at a Lebanese coffee house playing *thoule* (backgammon) and talking to the other men there. They all looked the same to me with white hair, white moustaches, suits, spats, and canes. No one spoke English, only Arabic. Sometimes Gido Ganem would bring his friends home for lunch or dinner. It never seemed to make a difference to Sitho; she always had lots of food ready all the time. Gido never talked to us. He would talk to Sitho or my mother, and they would talk to us for him. I guess he thought it wasn't his job.

Everybody else in the house talked to us all the time. We got orders and directions from all the adults. It was easier to just follow directions than to try to sort out who the real boss was. My mother simply did whatever kept the peace and counseled us to do the same.

When I was born, Sitho was fifty-two years old. She always seemed old, but also ageless. She married my Gido in Lebanon when she was fifteen. It was an arranged marriage as they all were at that time. They had five sons and two daughters, and two other babies died at birth. My father was the third child.

Gido always dressed in a suit, spats, shirt, and tie, and when he went out he wore a hat. In the summer, he wore a straw hat. Gido was short, but very neat looking with a well-trimmed moustache and classic Lebanese looks: dark eyes, a big nose, and full lips. The family's food business was called "Joseph Ganem and Sons," but I never remember him going to work.

Sitho wore only ordinary house dresses except when someone came to visit. At those times she always wore something black. Her hair was white and she wore it pulled back in a bun. She had a beautiful soft face and was the only one in the family with blue eyes.

She worked very hard all the time. When she woke up in the morning, she would pick up a dust rag and dust everything she passed on her way downstairs to the kitchen. She spent most of her day in the kitchen. There were anywhere from fifteen to twenty people in the house to feed at any given time. Many times there were guests for lunch or dinner, who were brought home by Gido or one of my uncles. Her daughters-in-law had assignments every day. Some did the laundry, some did the cleaning, some babysat the children, and each did a turn helping Sitho in the kitchen with the cooking.

Sitho didn't talk very much, except to her two daughters, with whom she was closest. She would ask for help softly and gently, *"Ya binthe, malamalouf,* ("My daughter, do me a favor."). No one ever said no to Sitho.

She must have had stories to share, complaints even about the work or her sons and daughters-in-law; how they helped or how they looked or dressed. Did she have favorites? Did she wish everyone would move out and leave her alone? Would she like just once to sleep late? Did Gido get on her nerves? No one knew what she thought except maybe her two daughters.

I loved Sitho's quietness. The younger women in the house, my mother and her sisters-in-law, seemed to talk all the time. They sometimes sang in English around Sitho so she could not understand. Something like, "I think I'll go shopping this afternoon, do you want to come with me? Don't stop working just sing me your answer and she'll never know. Maybe we can stop and have lunch. No one will know." Sitho didn't know the words, but my guess is she knew the gist of the song and didn't care.

Everything in the kitchen was big. The cabinets were big enough to hold huge pans. The shelves were deep enough to hold the place settings for twenty-four. But the biggest thing about the kitchen wasn't in the kitchen, it was down four steps between the kitchen and the laundry room. The Big House had a walk-in refrigerator. On the outside, it looked like a bank vault with a huge handle. It had a tile floor and six shelves on either side of it that ran up to the ceiling. Usually there were a couple of milk jugs on the floor. One held *leban* (yogurt) and the other held milk.

The shelves held crates of fruit. Depending on the season, sometimes there would be a crate of oranges, sometimes a crate of fresh figs. In the summer, there was always a whole watermelon.

Sitho made her own cheese, so there would be big glass bowls of cheese in brine. I don't know how it was made, but I remember what she did when she made it. She would sit on one chair with two chairs in front of her. One of the chairs had a big pan that contained the cheese. She would scoop out a handful of cheese; shape it into a flat, round patty; and put it in cheese cloth on the other chair. When she was finished, she would put all the patties in a bowl with brine to preserve them. She made kibbee balls using the same method, making them all the same size. She would take a handful of the ground lamb and bulgur wheat and begin to spin it in one hand while using the other hand to make a hollow in it for the stuffing. It looked easy, but no one else could do it.

In the spring, she would ask one of her daughters-in-law to drive her to the country to pick grape leaves by the side of the road. She would know just where to go to get the best ones. Sometimes she would take me with her to help. I didn't help much, but she would hand me those that she picked and I would take them back to the car. She didn't talk, but she would make sounds as she picked. I think they were Arabic words. They sounded soft and sweet to me.

No one went into Sitho's bedroom. The door was never open. Only once did I go in. She had asked me to go upstairs for her and get a brush from her bureau. I remember feeling nervous about opening the door. I knew the room was empty; Gido was at the coffee house, as always. The room was dark and cool, much cooler than the rest of the house. It smelled clean just like Sitho. There was nothing much in the room, except twin beds against two walls, one bureau, an oriental rug on the floor between the beds, and only a crucifix and a picture of Jesus on the wall. I grabbed the brush and ran out of the room.

Sitho knew how to fix just about everything. If one of us had an earache, she would heat some oil, put just a little in your ear, and then have you stay lying down for a few minutes so the oil could do its work and everything was fine. If we came in from the cold and our hands were numb, she would take them in hers, put them on her chest near her heart, and hold them there for a little while. In just a moment the heat from her body warmed our cold.

She was not always gentle. Her sons tried for years to convince her that chickens and turkeys were clean in the United States. She was never convinced and always killed her own chickens and turkeys before she cooked them. My father would take her to the farm, and she would pick out the bird or birds she wanted. The farmer would put them in a crate, and my father and Sitho would bring them home. Most often the birds would be in one of the garages for a day or two before Sitho needed them. She had a special cleaver for the birds. It was not a big deal for her. She was not afraid to do it, and no one helped. If her grandchildren were around and wanted to watch, that was all right with her. She just told us to stand back, away from her, while she did it. She did some muttering in Arabic that no one could hear or understand. She picked up the cage herself and brought it behind the house to a stump that was only used for that occasion. Without any wasted movement, she would open the cage, take the bird out with one hand on its neck and the other holding its legs. The bird would squawk and kick. But Sitho moved deliberately. Sitho put the neck of the chicken on the stump, took the cleaver, and with one big swipe, land it where she wanted it. The chicken's head was off, but the chicken's body would keep moving, wings fluttering and feathers flying. We saw the scene many times. It was just what Sitho did.

Chapter 2

The Kitchen

The kitchen was the heart of the Big House. Sitho spent most of her day in the kitchen; she gave it heart and warmth. She wore a white butcher apron. I think my father used to bring them home from the meat department for her. She was small, not even five feet tall, so the apron would have to be folded in front so the ties would be at her waist.

Just like every other room in the house, the kitchen was big. From the back door, the first part of the kitchen was a sitting room. It had a big leather couch and two big chairs. There was a built-in cabinet with glass doors that held some of the kitchen dishes and glasses. On the bottom shelf there were pictures of the old country that had to be looked at through a kind of three-dimensional viewer that gave the pictures some depth. I can remember looking at them once, but I never quite mastered the viewer—everything looked blurry.

There was a tile bathroom off the kitchen. The only adult in the family that ever used it was Uncle John. He was a lawyer and didn't have to go to work until nine o'clock. Everyone else was up and out by then. Uncle John would slick his hair with Vaseline until it was shiny and flat. No one else did that except for Uncle John. We all thought that lawyers had to have slick hair. He wore spats on his shoes, and we thought that was a lawyer thing, too. If he was feeling good, he would select one of us to button his spats with a special hook. He never asked the girls except Carol, his daughter. Other than Carol, he only asked the boys.

It was always good to see Uncle John leave for work. He got in the way of our fun.

The activity in the kitchen lasted all day. Breakfast started before 5:00 a.m. for the men involved in the business. They had to be up and out early to go to the wholesale houses in Boston to do the buying. My father often left at four in the morning to make the hour drive to the city. The main table in the kitchen was a long, specially designed table with benches that fit into a nook under some very large windows. Six people could sit on each bench. At the head of the table was a pass-through to the pantry. When everyone was there at once another table had to be added. This only happened on Sundays, and usually the dining room was used on that day.

As the house woke up, the kitchen filled up. The kids were the first after the men, except Uncle John. The women had to make sure that their children were fed and the older ones got off to school. There was always a bouncing chair in the kitchen with a baby in it.

Sitho was in the kitchen, making eggs in small fry pans and passing them through to the table, making coffee, and heating zathar bread and sweet sesame bread for anyone who wanted it. Lebanese cheese and leban (yogurt) were on the table, along with an assortment of black and green olives.

Somehow things flowed smoothly with everyone knowing their places at the table and what was expected. The women each had a job. Two of them cleaned up after the eating was over and two would begin the laundry duties. The laundry was down four steps off the kitchen in a small, L-shaped room attached to the garage. Between the kitchen and the laundry was the big walk-in refrigerator.

Sitho would begin cooking after the kitchen was cleaned up from breakfast.She would call one of us to her saying, "*Ya binthe, thi la houn*" ("My child, come here"). She would ask one of us to go to the walk-in refrigerator for something she needed for cooking.

Although Sitho never learned to speak English, she easily made herself understood to her grandchildren, who didn't speak Arabic. I can't quite describe how that worked, but we always knew what she was saying or what she was asking us to do. Even if she wanted to know what time it was, we knew to go into the front hall, look at the grandfather clock, and report back. In the afternoon, she always called either Aunt Margie or Aunt Blanche at work to talk to them. She never learned how to dial the telephone and would ask one of us to do it for her. The numbers were kept by the phone in the front hall, and she made it clear which one she wanted to call. It was special to be the dialer for Sitho.

There was a large family, the Quigleys, who lived on the street behind the Big House. There were eleven Quigleys and, at different times in our years at the Big House, almost all of the Quigley girls, six of them, worked at the Big House. They would come early afternoon and take care of some of us, taking us out for walks around the neighborhood or playing with us outside. Usually, two Quigleys worked at the same time; one took care of us and the other would help Sitho in the kitchen or help clean some part of the house. Sitho always sent some food home with them, patting them on the shoulder and saying some sweet blessing to them in Arabic that they didn't understand but appreciated just the same.

In the evening, the children in the family ate first, before the grownups, and it was very early, around five o'clock or earlier. I remember this because it was always in the middle of some kind of important play and there were shouts of protest from all of us.

"Just five more minutes, honest."

"Please, just one more thing."

The protests were not long. We knew the answer, but we had to ask anyway. There would be a little line in the bathroom off the kitchen to go to the toilet and wash our hands. No one cared about privacy, because we didn't know there could be any.

We ate at the table with mothers serving and supervising and an occasional push or shove from a cousin or sibling. The food we ate was always Lebanese. Sitho only cooked Lebanese food. We ate things like *cusa* (stuffed squash), *kibbeh* (ground lamb with bulgur wheat), and stuffed grape leaves or cabbage. I remember when my world grew beyond the Big House how much I liked other foods, such as baked beans and hot dogs.

We went to bed early. During the summer months, the sun would still be shining and we could hear the Quigleys on the back street still playing outside. My father was often not home from work before we went to bed, but when he was it was a special treat to see him and have him kiss me goodnight.

"Were you a good girl today?" Before I could answer, he answered for me, "Of course you were," and then he kissed me on the cheek. He smelled good.

Chapter 3

Patsy the Barber

I loved the barber shop. It smelled clean, like hair tonics and powders. I even liked the twirling sign in front of the shop. Mostly, I loved going there with my brothers, Billy and Allan, and having my hair cut. It was one of the sweet, simple times when there were no big decisions to make. My brothers had regular haircuts and I would get a Dutch cut. Patsy knew exactly what to do. Patsy always cut my hair, because that's what mother wanted. Sometimes Billy and Allan had Patsy's helper, Joe. Patsy owned the shop and he knew how to cut tricky hair like mine.

"Isn't her hair something else!" Mother would say. "Really much more like feathers than hair!".

"Oh, Adma, I love Jackie's hair. It has character, right, Jackie? You have character, and that's a good thing."

I had more fun at the barber shop when my mother just left us there and went somewhere else to do errands. When she was there she only talked to Patsy so she hung around my chair looking at me. She never said anything to Patsy about how he was cutting my hair, but Patsy talked to her instead of to me.

Haircut days were special. We first went to Patsy when we were still living with Sitho. My mother would drive to my father's market and park the car. We would stop at the market and see my father first. I think my mother had to get money from him for the haircuts. Everyone knew us and talked to us, especially to my mother. We could take anything we wanted from the market. I usually took a fresh donut from the donut-making machine that was always running. The donut flopped out warm, and I could roll it in sugar, cinnamon, or whatever I wanted. Adele was the donut lady, and she let me roll the donut many times to get as much sugar on it as I wanted. My mother was distracted with talking, so she couldn't tell me not to eat. This was a rare treat for me since she usually watched everything I ate.

Patsy's shop was just one block from the Big House on Amesbury Street. We walked there pushing and shoving each other for no reason except it was fun and annoyed my mother. I always thought Patsy knew we were coming and that he was waiting for us. If he was not cutting someone's hair, he would come outside with a towel in his hand and sweep it in front of himself as he bowed hello.

"Hey, lovely lady. Welcome to my shop," he said to me.

"You two guys, too," he said to Billy and Allan. When my mother had things to do she left us at the door with Patsy saying she would be back in an hour to pick us up. "Take your time Adma, these guys are no trouble."

Patsy had to put a special seat on the chair for me and help me up just a little. With the seat, I could see myself in the mirror, and I could also watch Patsy and everyone else in the shop. Sometimes Billy would be in the chair right next to me, staring at me and sticking his tongue out when no one was watching.

I loved the swish of the cape when Patsy shook it open to put around my neck. I liked the way I looked in the cape when I saw myself in the mirror. The buzzer would come out with a clean comb and scissors. He rubbed my head a little, just like Sitho would do. I liked the smell of the spray he put on my head. He buzzed the back of my head. I think that was part of the Dutch cut. He parted my hair many times and cut a little here and there. I never knew how he knew when he had finished. Had he cut enough? Was it too much? He just seemed to know he was done with the haircut. One of my favorite parts was the brush with the powder. The brush was big and Patsy would sprinkle powder on it and brush my neck, my chin, and then do a light brush all over my face.

"There you are, my beauty!" he would say with a flourish as he snapped the cape to shake the hair from it. I was sorry I had to get down from my perch. Billy and Allan were already finished with their haircuts, and there was nothing to keep us there. My mother was back and ready to pay Patsy for the three haircuts. I loved the smell of the powder and hoped it would last for a while but it never did. We put on our coats and said goodbye to Patsy and Joe.

Then we were out on the sidewalk again, pushing and shoving each other all the way back to the car. We picked up my father, so I was in the middle of the back seat. I never got a window seat unless there were only four of us in the car. I could still smell the powder from Patsy. We all smelled good in the back seat.

"How was Patsy?" my father asked.

"He's Patsy," my mother answered for us.

"That's a good thing," my father answered.

Chapter 4

Saturdays at the Big House

Saturdays were beautiful at the Big House. First of all, we never wondered who we would play with. There were always a few cousins in the house even if some were busy with parent things. In the spring and summer, the orchard behind the house was a great place to climb trees or pick peaches, apples, or pears. In the front of the house at the turn of the driveway was a huge mulberry tree that dropped its berries on the driveway and left a permanent purple stain year-round. The apples, pears, and peaches were picked for canning and eating, but the mulberries were left to fall on the ground. When the season was at its fullest, all of us kids in the family walked around with purple lips from eating the berries.

On Saturday, Sitho made fried eggs in small iron pans.

Each of us got our own fry pan of eggs, which were fried in oil and seasoned with *zathar*, a Lebanese spice. We ate them with Syrian bread right from the pan without forks or knives. How could anyone eat an egg with a fork? How do you get the yolk on the fork? There were some things we knew better than anyone else and how to eat fried eggs was one of them.

We went to the movies almost every Saturday afternoon. The movies went on for hours—usually a double feature, cartoons, and a serial feature. We always walked to the movies. It was over a mile away with only one street to cross. No one ever questioned our safety in walking. I never remember any grown up in the family admonishing us about being careful or the dangers of strangers.

The movie cost ten cents and candy cost five. We carried our own money. Once in a while, depending on who doled out the money, the oldest one in the group carried the money for all of us. No one liked that arrangement. There was usually a fight or two on the way to the movie with torments of candy denial if we didn't do what the keeper of the money ordered. The walk was probably twice as long as it needed to be, because we never walked directly to the movie theater. We stopped to pick up things along the way—just any old thing, like a buttercup to tickle under the chin, or a three-leaf clover that we made into a four-leaf clover. We never fooled anyone, but we always did it anyway. We passed a building on the way that had a double water outlet on the outside. I think it was for a fire hose hookup. We didn't know what it was for, but we always stopped there to push our hands inside and move the flapper in it from side to side. It made a great noise and all of us had to do it at least a few times before we moved on. We walked by a waterfall with a heavy wrought iron fence in front of it. We picked up sticks along the way for the sole purpose of running them along the fence. The fence begged to be tapped everytime we passed and we didn't disappoint.

When we did get to the theater, there was a line of kids waiting to get in. There was pushing and shoving and fights about who cut in front of whom. The same kind of crowd was in front of the refreshment stand inside. Hands were up in the air with nickels in each one, asking for their favorite candy bars. Sometimes you got what you wanted and sometimes you just took what was handed to you. Finding seats was a battle, too, moving from the back of the theater to the front. Some kids climbed over the seats. There were shouts back and forth between friends and a few punches here and there around the theater. Ushers tried to quiet the crowd, and there would be a lull in the action as they went up and down with flashlights, but then the noise would rise again. All this happened while the movies were playing. We watched what we could. It didn't matter; it was a great day anyway. The serial story was the last one to play. It was short and usually had cowboys and Indians chasing each other. At the end of the film was a scene with the good guy falling down a cliff, or off his horse, or just about to be hit with an arrow or shot by a gun. The whole crowd moaned at the close of the serial. Everyone wanted more. We filed out slowly, pushing and shoving, trying to put on jackets and hats in the cold weather. We went out to afternoon sun, squinting with blood shot eyes from hours in the dark. Now we had the long walk home.

No matter how late, we traced the same steps and same stops on the way home. We ran our sticks on the iron fence, we took turns moving the flapper back and forth inside the double water outlet, and we stopped for buttercups, pretend four leaf clovers, or fuzzy dandelions to blow at each other. We climbed the stone steps in front of the Big House, tired but happy with the day and the knowledge that the next Saturday would be just the same and just as much fun.

Chapter 5

Kindergarten

I went to Mrs. Cole's kindergarten when I was five. Mrs. Cole had a helper, Miss Pingree. Kindergarten was not required in those days, but my mother thought I should get started and, anyway, it would be one less child in the house for a couple of hours. I liked kindergarten. It was easy, it had a routine, and I always liked routine. Mr. Cole, Mrs. Cole's husband, drove right to the Big House to pick me up every day. He drove up the driveway and stopped right in front of the back kitchen door. Everyone in the kitchen waved to me through the window. I sat in the front seat with Mr. Cole. He smoked cigars and smelled like Uncle Bill.

The girls had dolls and a big doll house. We also had pretend tea cups and dishes. The boys had blocks and trucks. They could run all around the room, but we had to stay with the dolls in the corner. Every time I went to play with the blocks, Miss Pingree told me to go back with the girls where I belonged.

We had to line up for the toilet after we played for a while. The toilets were small and low to the floor. I never once went to the toilet there. Miss Pingree would tell me that I had to go.

"But I don't have to go."

"Yes you do, now just go in and go."

"I don't have to."

"Yes, yes you do!"

So I would go in, pretend I went, and flush the toilet—but I never did go. I was afraid of the toilet and afraid of Miss Pingree.

After the toilet we washed our hands and sat down at long tables for snack time. We had graham crackers and milk every day. I had never had graham crackers and thought they were delicious. At the Big House we never had store-bought cookies; we had only Lebanese sweets that Sitho made. I liked the graham crackers better than any of the sweets she made. We had rest time on the floor with blankets we brought from home. We didn't really rest, we just lay there and whispered and poked each other. I loved the smell of the floor. The last part of the day was story time. Mrs. Cole always did the reading. Once in a while she would ask us to tell a story. I was the only one who lived with grandparents, uncles, aunts, and cousins, so Mrs. Cole asked me to talk about my family. I remember telling the class about Sitho.

"What's a Sitho?"

"Ya, what's a Sitho?"

"I don't have a Sitho."

I only knew the word Sitho; I didn't know the word grandma or gram or nana.

"Well, I think you mean grandmother." Mrs. Cole said.

"No, no I don't, I mean Sitho. I don't have a grandma, I have a Sitho."

"What does a Sitho do?" she asked.

"Sitho cooks all our food. She cooks *kibbee* and *lubee* and *imjaddarah* and sometimes she makes *bitlawa* (a Lebanese sweet)."

The kids laughed and pointed at me.

"You're all stupid," I said and I sat down. *I'm not going to talk again in this place*, I thought to myself. And I didn't. Mrs. Cole gave up the Sitho questions and didn't ask me again for a story about home.

There was a girl in my class whose name was Betty Juba. My father knew Betty's father, Mike. He was an electrician. He used to pick Betty up in his truck with the sign that said, "JUBA ELECTRIC.". Betty's mother and father were divorced. We didn't know what that meant, but we saw that it made Betty very unhappy. Betty cried almost every day at school. I remember thinking divorce must be a very bad thing. It set Betty apart from everyone else. Miss Pingree and Mrs. Cole treated Betty differently. Betty could play whatever she wanted or nothing at all. When Mr. Juba came to pick Betty up, he whispered with Mrs. Cole. No one wanted to be with Betty or even stand next to her. At rest time, Betty didn't lie down on the floor with a blanket, she sat in a chair.

At Christmas, Sitho made a special batch of bitlawa for me to give to Mrs. Cole and Miss Pingree. My mother wrapped them in Christmas paper. Mrs. Cole and Miss Pingree loved the present.

"That bitlawa is delicious. Do you think I can get the recipe from your mother?" Mrs. Cole asked. She still didn't understand that the bitlawa was from my Sitho.

"My Sitho doesn't use recipes," I said, "She doesn't need them, she just knows how to make everything without the recipes."

They never did understand about Sitho.

Chapter 6

Moving Out

In 1941, we had to move out of The Big House. My mother had another baby, my sister Mimi (Miriam), and Sitho said there was not enough room in the Big House for all of us. We would miss the Big House. In some ways it was easy living there. We always had someone to play with. We had a very big yard, garage, and basement filled with things to explore—not the usual toys, but big old meat cases, large roll-top oak desks, oak file cabinets filled with ledger paper ready for us to draw on, and furniture from the old country that was carefully covered for protection. There were also floor lamps with dangly beads around the shades. Most of the colors of the furniture were dark: dark maroon, dark green, dark blue. There were water pipes with painted designs on the glass bottoms. Those colors were dark, too, but looked lighter because of the glass. The long tubes for the pipes had fancy looking ribbons hanging from them. When I smell a musty cellar, I think about those wonderful things in the basement of the Big House.

We celebrated all holidays and everyone's birthday. This meant that almost all year long we were celebrating something. There were at least one or two birthdays a month and then Christmas, New Year's eve and day, the Fourth of July, Valentine's Day. Christmas and the Fourth of July were my favorites.

Workers from the family business would come to the house weeks before Christmas and decorate the huge pine trees in front of the house. They had to use extension ladders to reach the tops. They would string lights around the front of the house, too. When it was all done, we all went out the first night to watch the lighting. It was not simple, because

18

if one light went out on a string, they all went out. For the weeks that the house was decorated, almost every day some repair work had to be done. I don't know what the neighbors thought. The traffic increased in front of the house. Cars slowed down and sometimes even stopped. It was a brilliant display.

The Fourth of July was almost as spectacular as Christmas. My grandfather had some of his helpers come to the house to set off a shower of fireworks. It seemed to go on for hours. We sat on the front steps and on the stone wall around the driveway. Between displays, we ate strawberries, drank lemonade, and pushed and poked each other just for the fun of it.

The toughest part of living in the Big House was following the directions of all of the grown ups. It was like having ten parents instead of two. Any one could boss you around. One of my aunts was not Lebanese, her name was Emma. She was English. She did not like the arrangement one bit. She let everyone know that she was the mother of her children and no one else could tell them what to do. Sometimes she would take her kids and stay in her two rooms with them all day. Hers was the first family to move out. I don't think anyone missed her.

You would think that having ten parents would be harder than having two; it was not. I don't remember my mother much at the big house. She sort of did what she was told, just like we did.

Life was easier for my mother when we moved to Canterbury Street in Andover, Massachusetts. She was twenty-one when she married my father. She felt tremendous pressure to do the right thing all the time. She wanted to be the best daughter-in-law in the house. She was pushed and pulled in every direction trying to please everyone except those closest to her, her children and husband. We were hers, no matter what, but the others needed winning over.

In the Lebanese community, my father was considered a "great catch." This put more stress on my mother to prove she was a good wife and mother. She did her very best to accommodate everyone in the house, including my grandparents, and my father's older brothers. What they thought and what they wanted was my mother's first consideration. If discipline was meted out by them to one of us, it was okay with her. We just went with the flow of the day. We knew we were supposed to be good and being good was following directions from all the adults in the house.

When we moved to Andover, everything changed. One good thing was that I had my own room. I was eight and until we moved, I had shared a very large room with my two brothers where we each had our own bed and dresser. It was easy for my mother, too. She could sing us all to sleep at one time. I liked that. If any one of us had to go to the bathroom in the middle of the night, we had to use a potty that my mother had stationed at the doorway. I never went in the middle of the night. I was afraid to use that thing. My brothers used it all the time.

My mother seemed to have a lot more time in the new house. She had time to focus on me. Everything was important: what I wore, what I ate, how I walked, and what I did in school. Oh, and she had this thing about the sun. The sun was our enemy. "Never sit in the sun. You're dark enough," she would say. The sun was no good for any of us but especially for me, a girl. She had her own rules, a long list of do's and don'ts. There was no way to argue with them. Our list was different from other people's list, we were Lebanese for one thing. That meant we had olive skin. "So what?" you might say. The "*so what*" was that we were not like everyone else in the neighborhood, and maybe that meant we were less American. Being less American was not a good thing in my mother's book.

In Andover, we were the only Lebanese. Of course, we had some crazies on the street that made matters worse for my mother. Mrs. Merchant, two doors down, had a brogue so heavy almost no one understood her.

"Now, Annie," she would say to her daughter, "I don't want you playin' with the foreigner down the street."

That foreigner would be me. I didn't care; my mother cared. I would rather play with the boys anyway. And I did.

That first winter we were in Andover we had some great snow for sledding. We had a sledding place behind our house called Spy Tree Hill. It had the best sledding in the neighborhood. It was early, around 4:30 p.m., but getting dark. It would probably have been my last run of the day. It was a tricky place to sled because you had to weave your way through the trees. It was a path, sort of, but really only because we called it one. I think I might have been a show-off with my boy buddies, because I did everything they did, even if I had never done it before. I went flying down Spy Tree Hill and got about halfway down and smacked into a tree. The blood was all over me in just a few seconds.

It didn't hurt but the blood flow was scary. My Flexible Flyer sled was smashed. Some of the boys took off, fast. My brothers probably wanted to, but didn't. They knew mother would be furious at the whole thing.

She was more than angry; she was a frightened. She cleaned up my face and then we could see I had a cut down the center of my nose. It was not a big deal. It healed, but it healed with dirt under the skin. So I ended up with a black line down the center of my nose. It doesn't sound too bad, but to a mother like mine who was trying desperately for perfection, it was not good.

My mother got the name of a plastic surgeon from my Uncle JY, the doctor. I think his name was Dr. Simon. Anyway, Dr. Simon did the best he could, cutting open the scar and cleaning it out. But the best could do still left some soot under the skin. We tried creams and things, but it was still there. Actually, it is still there, but time has played its magic and faded the line.

My mother was not content to leave it alone. The following summer she decided that maybe if I could get a sunburn on my nose and have the skin peel, the scar would disappear. She cut a white sheet into a square to cover my face and cut an oblong hole in it just the size of my nose. We had a summer cottage in those days on a lake in southern New Hampshire. I spent many hours lying in the rowboat anchored in the middle of the lake with the stupid sheet on my face. I didn't want anyone to see me. It is the only time I can remember that my mother was okay with me being in the sun. At the end of the summer I had a very brown nose and a very white face. My skin did not burn, it did not peel. I looked freaky. Like it or not, olive skin does not burn.

Without the distraction of the other members of the family, my mother could focus on her children, mostly me. My sister was a baby and not yet ready for any remedial work. Billy and Allan were boys and had that inherent advantage that needs no fixing.

Every day at breakfast before school, my mother would shout, "Go take a look at yourself in the full length mirror!" I never knew what I was supposed to look at or for. As a matter of fact, I never looked at myself. I would get up, go to the mirror stand for a minute, and then go back to my toast and jam. I was supposed to see how fat I was and stop eating. I didn't see anything and I liked to eat. My two brothers ate even more than I did, but she said nothing to them. They were okay, and I was not.

My mother was uncomfortable in this new community. We had to try to be like everyone else, to fit in. The children in Andover took lessons—all kinds of lessons. So we took lessons: fencing, elocution, piano, violin, ballet, swimming, and ballroom dancing. There was no place to hide in our house in Andover, no big garages, no big utility sheds, and no basement. There was no Sitho, either.

I could escape to my own room by myself when I needed to get away. I had my own special fantasy life there. I could pretend that I was tall, thin, and beautiful. I sent away for every weight-loss package I could find on the back of my brother's comic books, mostly pills and plungers. The plunger was just like a toilet plunger except smaller. It came with instructions on how to use it. It was called a "spot reducer" and was to be used in the bathtub. The instructions read, "Place the moist plunger on your stomach and press until suction is created. Pull plunger off with a quick, brisk movement. Repeat until the desired amount of fat is removed."

What the advertisements never told you was that along with the tools and pills, you also had to go on a diet. If you had a good breakfast that was about all the food you could have for the day. I would diet for about two days and use the plunger until the skin on my stomach was red and raw. With all that pain, I had to be thinner. I wasn't turning any heads yet, and I had to make sure no one saw me naked until the plunger scars disappeared, but I was sure I looked better.

Graymoor monastery in upstate New York advertised on the radio: "Send a donation and we will pray for you. We will pray for your special intentions. "

"Please, please help me lose weight," I wrote.

The monks received my donation. I know because they sent me a thank you receipt. I waited for several days, even weeks. Nothing happened. In the meantime, I looked in the hallway full-length mirror when my mother told me to and continued to eat my toast and jam. The remedies required faith and discipline. I didn't have either one. I loved my mother very much, but she didn't make it easy. I worked very hard to please her, but never could. If I did please her in any way, she never let me know.

When I was fourteen years old, I went away to Kendall Hall, a private school in Peterborough, New Hampshire. That was a good thing for me, and I supposed it was a good thing for my mother, too. She could put her quest for my thinness on hold except for vacation times. But before I left in September, I had to endure the anguish of going clothes shopping with her. I never liked shopping for clothes or the humiliation of trying things on that didn't fit. I was embarrassed to hear what size dress or blouse I took. It was painful to watch my mother's face as I modeled the new things

My father had reached a level of success in business that allowed my mother to shop at the fanciest boutiques around. We didn't have the anonymity of a department store with racks of clothes to browse in solitude. These places had no clothes on display. The sales person looked at me and brought those things she thought were suitable—after, of course, a discussion with my mother. No one asked me what I wanted. Truth be told, I didn't want anything except to leave and go home alone. My mother's favorites were Rose Frank's Dress Salon and The Vogue, which was owned by Ida Tattelman.

Ida and Rose both had the same approach. They would watch my mother for her reaction to the clothes and say, "Darling, I wouldn't let you leave the shop without this. It is stunning!" or, "It is not you; take it off."

I never knew what I wanted and my mother never asked me what I wanted. I remember being in awe of my friends who actually knew what they liked. Even if their mothers didn't like the same things, they fought for it until they got what they wanted. Not me. There I would stand, not looking, not speaking, and not caring. "Put this on; put that on; take that off; stand up straight; put your head up!"

The biggest joke of all was when I was asked, "Do you like this dress?"

"Do you want that suit?"

"Do you like this color?"

Standing on a platform in front of a three-way mirror, I am actually supposed to look at myself and like what I see? It was three times the torture of the full-length mirror in the hall. Could I look? If I looked, could I see? Mostly I said, "Yes, it's okay, do you like it Mom?"

Actually, none of it made any difference. When I left for school in September with my new clothes, my mother never knew whether I wore them or not. We had uniforms for every day, so the new, expensive clothes stayed in the closet until I went home for vacation.

Chapter 7

Growing up on Canterbury Street

Our house on Canterbury Street was perfect for kids. We had a big back yard, an open field beyond a row of huge pine trees, and Spy Tree Hill behind that. It was a neighborhood full of kids, although only three were girls. Barbara Bird was a little older than I was and Ann Merchant was a little younger than I was. I didn't care because I wanted to play with the boys anyway. I liked the games the boys played. One game they played was "war." This was during the time of World War II. It was the good guys, the Americans, against the bad guys. It was me and the boys. We even dug fox holes in the field and covered them over with camouflage. Billy Dean fell into one of the holes and broke his ankle. We had to take the camouflage away after that.

The games we played always started and ended in a fight. It started in a fight because picking sides was never easy. First of all, in the beginning, no one wanted me on their team. I was a girl. Then, no one really wanted to be on the bad guy's side, because they always lost. At the end of the game, there was a fight over who was dead and who was not.

"I shot you first."

"No way, I saw you first and shot you with my machine gun!"

Sometimes there were pushes and shoves back and forth. There was always a lot of yelling and screaming. I loved it.

In the warm weather, the boys took off their shirts and played bare-chested. I took my shirt off and my mother saw me out the kitchen window and ran out to get me.

"What are you doing, Jackie! For God's sake, girls don't run around outside without their shirts. Bad enough you play with the boys all the time. You put your shirt on right this minute and don't let me see you without it again. Understand? What next . . ." she went on and on and on.

"Ha, ha, Jackie, na, na, na na na." My brother Allan usually led the chorus when I returned.

I never stopped taking my shirt off when the boys did, I just didn't do it where my mother could see me.

In the basement of that house we had a play room. It was nothing fancy, but it was someplace we could go do what we wanted to do and not care if the place got dirty. Every Christmas we would get one thing that totally took over the playroom. The one I remember best was a plaster craft set that made heads of the presidents. The heads were rubber molds that we would fill with plaster and let harden. Then we would paint them. I know my mother thought. "Here's a good thing for them. They can make things and learn about the presidents at the same time." She was always looking to improve us. Of course, we didn't care about the presidents. We only cared about making the heads, how many of each we had, which ones were the best, and which ones had bubbles in them where the plaster missed a space. There were lots of rules about which ones were best. One of the big collector items was Abe Lincoln without his left ear. We made heads, heads, and more heads for months. Allan had the best display for his heads. He had a big shelf over his bed. He had about thirty heads on it in all different colors. The next Christmas after we started making the heads, Allan put lights all around the shelf. We thought it was a great show piece. All through the year the three of us used the heads to barter. Some Saturdays we would display those heads that could be bartered on the beds in each of our bedrooms.

"I'll trade you two Washington's for one Abe Lincoln," Billy would say to Allan.

Of course, Allan had the best display, so all of his looked better than Billy's or mine. Allan only had one or two that he was willing to trade. Billy had a whole bunch, but he thought more about how many he could get. He didn't care about how they looked. Mine were the worst of the three displays. They usually had cracks or bubbles. There was a trick to filling the rubber molds that I never quite got. Allan was the best at it; it had to do with something about tapping the mold.

We would go back and forth. Those presidents' heads got handled by all of us all afternoon. A few of mine broke from the activity. They were fragile to begin with and couldn't take the rough handling. In the end, Allan still had the best collection. Billy had the most, of course, and I had the cracked and bubbled collection.

We had moved to Canterbury Street just in time to start school in September at the Shawsheen School. I was in Miss McCarthy's third grade class. My brother Billy was in the fifth grade and Allan was in the second grade.

I didn't like or dislike school, but I don't think Miss McCarthy liked me even though I never caused any trouble. Acting out was not anything I would have done. I was "there, but not there." I remember not caring about anything. The only time I ever had any feelings at school was when we would have to line up for something. We always lined up by size and I was always one of the big girls at the back of the line. Connie Medollo was the only one bigger than me and she was alot bigger. I felt like everyone was laughing at me. "Ha, Ha, you have to stand next to Connie." I felt the whispers behind my back like little stabs between my shoulders.

We went home every day for lunch. We walked in ordered groups with a patrol captain keeping us in line. Billy was a patrol captain. It made me feel special to have a brother as a captain. This good feeling never lasted very long, because Billy usually found some reason to boss me around.

Lunch was tricky. I never liked the Lebanese food my mother made for lunch. If there was a choice, I always took something other than Lebanese food. Peanut butter was a favorite. I don't think mother cared as long as I didn't eat much. My brothers could eat whatever they wanted.

Sometimes my father would pick us up from school at lunchtime and come home with us to eat. I loved that. If my mother said anything to me about eating, he would say, "Oh, Adma, leave her alone. She's okay." I always felt safe with my father around. When he said, "She's okay," it felt like a warm hug.

Midway through the school year, there was the usual Parents' Night at school. My mother never missed those, although my father never went to one. I imagine Miss McCarthy couldn't wait to talk to mother. She said, "Mrs. Ganem, Jackie sits here. This is her desk," pointing to my seat near the window in the back of the room. "All she does is sit here all day long and roll her pencil down the desk while she looks out the window. That's it. That's all she does."

I hated Miss McCarthy for that. For the rest of the school year I heard nothing else from my mother but, "Now don't just sit there and look out the window. What's the matter with you anyway? Your brothers don't do that. Billy is a patrol captain and Allan is singing in the school play."

Big deal. Of course, my brothers thought the whole thing was very funny. It wasn't funny for me. I had to listen to my mother every day. I couldn't wait for the end of the school year. Billy said that Miss Thurston, the fourth grade teacher, was much nicer than Miss McCarthy. She looked nicer. She smiled at me a few times. Miss McCarthy never smiled. The only time she smiled at me the whole year was when I brought butter for her from my father's market. Butter was hard to get during the war. I didn't want to bring it to her. I remember telling my father that I didn't like her and didn't want to give her anything. He smiled at me and said, "Give it to her, Jackie. It will make your life a lot easier." It did make life easier. I got all A's and B's, but I still didn't like her.

Chapter 8

Visits to the Big House

Sitho's grown children never left the house without first kissing her good bye. When they came home at night they kissed her hello. It was what we were all used to doing and seeing. The memory is a sweet one. Even after we moved out of the Big House we would visit every Sunday for dinner. My father was the first one to greet Sitho with a kiss and an Arabic blessing, "my beautiful boy'." The rest of us followed to kiss her too. Sitho would give us a blessing and repeat my father's name. The way she said it was beautiful. It didn't sound like Elias at all, but something more flowing and gentle.

I loved those Sunday dinners. Everyone was there. There was lots of talk among the adults. The women all pitched in to help with the dinner. The men sat in the living room and talked business and politics. The rest of the house was ours to explore. The basement continued to have new things to check out. There were always boxes of pictures and other treasures. We never knew who the people in the pictures were. We figured they were relatives from Lebanon that we didn't know. There was a second garage on the property that always had good things to look at, too. Games of hide-and-seek were endless, because finding anyone was impossible. Sometimes those of us who were hiding would just present ourselves, tired of hiding and maybe a little afraid, too.

In the evening after the dishes had been washed and put away, we would all gather in the living room around the piano. Aunt Blanche played the piano. She could play anything you wanted her to play. We just had to hum a few bars and she would take over. She never had a music lesson; she just knew how to play. She had a jerky way of playing. Her head was always moving up and down, side to side. Aunt Blanche was nicest when she was playing the piano. Most of the time, even though she had a smile on her face, we knew she wasn't happy. She loved Sitho and Aunt Margaret, but I don't think she liked her brothers very much. Her brothers didn't include her or Aunt Margaret in any conversations about the business or anything else for that matter. Even the children in the family got much more attention than they did. Aunt Margaret was very short. There were stories about why she was so short.

"Sitho didn't feed her because she was too busy."

"Sitho didn't feed her because she was a girl."

"She had a funny sickness that made her stop growing."

I couldn't believe Sitho would be that mean to her baby. Sitho loved Aunt Margaret and talked to her more than anyone else in the family except maybe Aunt Blanche. Aunt Margaret was happier than Blanche. She liked us better than Blanche did and she was more fun than Aunt Blanche, even though she didn't play the piano. Aunt Margaret would sometimes take her nieces up to her room on the third floor and let us pick out a piece of jewelry from her jewelry box. I didn't care too much about jewelry, but we felt so special when she invited us that the jewelry became something to treasure.

The Ganems were very serious people. Music must have seemed frivolous to them. They did have some talent and could have had great fun with music if they would let themselves have fun at all. My father had a wonderful singing voice, and when he was a young man, he sang in a barber shop quartet. That is, until Gido found out and he quickly put an end to it. "You're not working hard enough if you have time for that!" Gido would say in Arabic.

At some of those Sunday get-togethers, my father would sing. I remember feeling like this was another man inside my father. His voice was deep and smooth. If it was a full-blown talent night, we would all have to do something to show off what lessons we were taking. Everyone was polite and clapped after each show, but then there was a lot of chuckling and talking in Arabic that followed.

My cousin Elaine was a tap dancer. She had regular tap shoes with the big noisy taps on the toes and heels. I would have loved a pair of those. One of the small rugs would be rolled up and Aunt Blanche would play the piano for Elaine to dance. She was a great hit.

My cousin Carol usually read a story or had memorized a poem to recite. She did it with great flare.

My brother Billy and I took violin lessons. My brother Allan took piano lessons. So on talent night, we played a trio. Billy and I hated it, but Allan liked it. He knew a little bit more than Billy and I did about what we were doing. There was no getting out of it. We just had to get it done. Everyone clapped and laughed a lot. Sitho didn't laugh as much as everyone else. She smiled.

It would seem like midnight when we finished, but it would only be about seven or eight in the evening. Everyone would go to the coat closet and scramble for their coats. Winter meant boots and mittens and hats. Sitho would stay seated in her chair, and we would line up again to kiss her good bye and thank her. It seemed to take forever to get out with everyone doing the same thing at the same time. Even backing out of the driveway was tricky. Sometimes it meant sitting in the car and waiting for the car behind to back out first.

Chapter 9

Kendall Hall

I'm not sure why my parents chose Kendall Hall for me. I think it was because I had two cousins, Carol (Uncle John's daughter) and Joyce (my mother's sister Malvina's daughter), who were going there and that made it easy. I was not asked what I wanted. Like always, the expectation was that I would go with whatever was decided.

Kendall Hall was on 350 acres of beautiful land between Mount Monadnock and Pack Monadnock. There were beautiful pine covered hills, open fields, and dirt roads with small outbuildings used for different activities. The main house held the dining hall, library, offices, infirmary, and dormitory rooms for all of the underclassmen. The house was set on a hill. On one side was a view of Mount Monadnock and on the other side there was a view of Pack Monadnock. Beyond the French doors in the library was a rose garden, the pride and joy of Ernie the groundskeeper. Down six stone steps was an old in-ground pool that was seldom used but fun to sit by. The library was lined floor-to-ceiling with books. It was also used as the school auditorium and music room.

There was a wonderful order to the school, and it was a great comfort in knowing exactly what was expected all the time. Every day had a schedule. We woke up at the same time; had breakfast at the same time; had classes at the same time; ate lunch and dinner at the same time; and the same was true for various activities and study hall every day. I remember that some girls didn't like the order. They complained or just didn't follow the schedule.

The school was very small with only 60 girls in attendance. It was not a place you could hide, but on the other hand, it was not tough to shine. I think I really did shine there. I was the same acquiescing, insecure person on the inside, but on the outside I was someone else. I was smart. I volunteered for everything. I was good at all sports, and was in all the plays we produced. I was assistant editor, and then editor, of our school paper. I even made the finals in the statewide speech contest. Almost everyone was a friend. I forgot about being fat.

Not long ago when I moved, some friends were helping with unpacking pictures and we came across some old ones of me at Kendall Hall. My friend, Mariann, said,

"I thought you told me you were fat when you were a kid, you're not fat, look at this!"

I did look and surprise of all surprises, I was not fat. How did that happen? I decided that the fat thing was so much part of me that I never thought I could be anything else but fat.

In that small, girls' private school in Peterborough, I had the best teacher I ever had in all of my school years, including college and graduate school. She was the wife of the headmaster, George Kendall. We called them Mr. and Mrs. George to distinguish them from Mr. George's parents who were the founders of the school. She taught English and gave me a lifelong love of the language and an appreciation of good writing. She introduced me to the *New York Times*, which I have read ever since. My world grew and I began to see what was possible.

Barbara Ferguson was my best friend at Kendall Hall. She was from New York City. When I was fifteen, she invited me to go home with her for spring vacation. I got permission from home. Her parents were divorced and Barbara's mother was remarried to a man much younger than she was. Barbara had one sister, Janet, who was a fashion model in the city. They lived on Fifth Avenue across from the Metropolitan Museum of Art in a building that had a doorman and an elevator man.

On the first night of our visit, Barbara's father was cutting up one steak to feed all of us. That was different. In my family, we each got a steak that looked like the one Mr. Ferguson was cutting up for the whole family. Something didn't compute. I guessed that the Fergusons would rather pay for the maid to serve them than to get more food. Or maybe if you lived on Fifth Avenue across from the Metropolitan Museum like the Fergusons did, with a doorman and an elevator man, you had to have a maid.

Mr. Ferguson had picked us up at Grand Central Station. He was tall and handsome. He looked like he could be Barbara's boyfriend more than her step-father. I was never certain what he did for a living. I definitely knew it was nothing like my father did. He wore a suit, went to an office in the Graybar building, and traveled all over the world. That's about all she said about her family. She didn't say whether she liked them or didn't like them.

The dinner was quiet, nothing like my house. Mr. Ferguson did most of the talking. Mrs. Ferguson didn't eat anything on her plate. Janet ate just a little and asked to be excused. Barbara and I ate everything. I asked if I could help with the dishes. Barbara kicked me under the table and the maid came out of the kitchen and whisked everything away.

We never saw Barbara's mother very much during the vacation. She seemed to sleep most of the day. Barbara would go into her bedroom and tell her what we were going to do for the day and we would leave. I would peek in, but never saw much except pillows and blankets. I never asked Barbara why her mother stayed in bed all day and she never told me. This was certainly different from the mother I knew. My mother was always up early and made sure everyone else was, too. She always had a full day, mostly revolving around her four children and our activities, except for her shopping, cooking, and cleaning.

The one time during the week that I spent any time with Mrs. Ferguson was when Barbara had a dentist appointment late one afternoon. Mrs. Ferguson came out of her bedroom and asked me if I wanted to get a drink with her at a bar around the corner. I don't know what I thought at the time, but I do remember thinking it would be rude to say "No, thank you," so I said yes.

She looked tired and a little puffy around the eyes. *Maybe it is from sleeping so much*, I thought. We went down to the lobby of the building. Both the elevator man and the doorman asked Mrs. Ferguson how she was feeling. Barbara had not told me that her mother was sick, but it did figure since she slept so much.

The bar was right around the corner. It had a dark maroon canopy in front of the door and a doorman, too. This was the very first time I had been in a bar. I remember thinking to myself, *okay you are only sixteen and the drinking age is eighteen*. As a matter of fact, I wasn't even sure it was legal for me to be in there even with Mrs. Ferguson. Well, no one looked at me and no one said anything to me about not being allowed, so I just followed Mrs. Ferguson. Everyone knew her and called her by name.

"How are you, today?"

"Haven't seen you in a while."

"How good to see you."

"Would you like your usual table and usual drink?"

I had always looked older than I was, so no one asked if I was old enough to drink. Mrs. Ferguson just assumed I would drink with her.

"What would you like, dear?" She asked me.

The big thing was, of course, not to act like you were a newcomer to the scene. *Just spit something out,* I thought. I had heard people order different drinks in the movies, so I picked one.

"I'll have a rye and ginger, thank you," I answered, like I knew what I was doing and had done it many times before. I didn't have a clue what a rye and ginger was, but I knew it sounded good. Mrs. Ferguson's usual was a martini.

I felt good sitting there with low lights and soft music playing. I smoked cigarettes at that time and of course that made me fit right in. Everybody smoked. I offered Mrs. Ferguson a cigarette, put one in my mouth, and lit them both. This was great. I crossed my legs, leaned back a little, and tried to make conversation with Mrs. Ferguson. She didn't like to talk much. I wished Barbara were with me; maybe she could get the conversation going. Finally, the drinks arrived.

My drink looked simple enough, like a ginger ale. I picked it up and took a small sip. *Oh, my god, this is terrible,* I thought. *Don't make a face, you jerk.* Mrs. Ferguson took two large sips and smiled. "That's better," she said. She took two more sips, the drink was almost gone, and the waiter brought another without her asking for it. She was getting a little chattier now.

"Drink up, Jackie. Karl, bring my friend another drink."

"I'll have a whiskey sour this time," I said. I remember thinking that it might taste better than this rye and ginger thing I had in front of me. Mrs. Ferguson and Karl gave me a quizzical look, but we moved ahead with no questions asked. *I really wish Barbara was here.* I thought. *Well, okay, here comes the drink. Oh good, it has some cherries and orange slices in it. It was a good choice.* I ate the cherries and the orange slices as I was getting a little hungry. Mrs. Ferguson had a third drink and was more talkative. I don't remember what she was talking about. It didn't seem to require any answers from me or, for that matter, any participation at all.

Finally, after I don't know how long, Barbara and her father walked in and right up to the table, like they knew exactly where to find us. Neither one of them looked at me at first. They looked at Mrs. Ferguson. Then Mr. Ferguson looked at Karl and said, "Karl, put the bill on my account, thanks." It didn't sound friendly, but it didn't sound angry either.

"Jackie, are you all right?" he asked.

"Oh, sure I am. I'm fine," I said, wondering why he would ask. Of course I was all right, just a little hungry. The orange slices and cherry didn't do much to fill me up. Barbara looked pale. Maybe it was something the dentist did.

"Are you okay, Barbara?" I asked.

"I'm fine now," she answered.

We all left the bar. Mr. Ferguson held Mrs. Ferguson's arm and took her up to the apartment. I guessed she wasn't hungry. Barbara and I waited in the lobby of the building. In about ten minutes, Mr. Ferguson came down the elevator. He looked a little better and Barbara did, too.

He put one arm around me, the other around Barbara and kissed us both on the head.

"O.K. you two, what will it be, Chinese or Italian?" he asked.

The Family

Chapter 10

Elias Louis Ganem

My father was born in 1901. I loved my father. We had a very special connection, a kind of powerful, unspoken affinity. It isn't anything you can see and it isn't anything you can describe. It just is. He was not the kind of man who would spend any time thinking about these things. There was not an analytical bone in his body. He was, in that sense, a very simple man. He didn't think about why people did what they did or felt what they felt. His world was the here and now.

My father was a short, overweight man. When anyone asked him how tall he was, he would say he was 5' 6" but we all knew he was 5' 3", maybe 5' 3 ½". When he was asked about how tall a friend or colleague was, he would say, "He's a big guy like me."

I'm 5' 6" and have been that height since I was twelve years old. In all of the pictures of us standing together, it was clear that I was taller than he was. This fact never changed his mind or his perception of himself. I always thought of him as big and powerful, and even now I look at some of those pictures and can feel surprise at how short he really was.

Most people liked my father very much. There was an endearing, naïve quality about him that seemed to fly in the face of his shrewdness. His simplicity pulled those qualities together so that he could relate to all kinds of people. The people who worked for him saw this immigrant simplicity as inspiration for them. Business people at all levels were drawn to his shrewd mind and great drive.

He quit school after the eighth grade. He didn't like it and couldn't wait to get involved with the work of making money. He simplified the world around him. He also simplified his name. Louie would be easier for everyone to remember. Elias was foreign–sounding. He became E. Louis Ganem, but his mother always called him Elias.

It was fun being Louie's daughter. During the World War II, all kinds of food items were almost impossible to get. Everyone had ration stamps for different things. For instance, a married couple might have a stamp for one pound of butter a month. Of course, you would have to find a grocer who had the butter to sell. Meat was hard to get, just like coffee, cigarettes, stockings, and gas.

Because my father was in the food business, we always had what we needed. Special friends could also get what they needed from us. Our teachers would ask my mother to ask my father for coffee or butter, and then we would carry little brown bags to school for them. My brothers, sister, and I felt special delivering the brown bags. Mostly, we all got all A's.

Sometimes on Saturdays, we would go to one of the markets and help out. My brothers would be in the meat department. The meat department was for boys only. No women worked there. Women were in the bakery department. I spent most of the time with cookies. It was not a busy department. I don't think they needed anyone there, but I got to wear a white jacket and printed on the front pocket was: "Ganem's Market. The Largest, Cleanest, Busiest Market in New England." I was supposed to wear a hat, but I hated it and never put it on. Everyone was nice to us all the time. Once in a while my father would show up in the afternoon. He would seem surprised to see us and even more surprised to see me with the cookies. He always asked for a hermit cookie.

My brothers were expected to work every summer, all summer. When I was fourteen and went away to school. I stopped working in cookies, even in the summer. I would have loved going with my brothers every day and doing whatever they did. I don't remember why I didn't work there in the summers. I think my mother thought it wasn't a ladylike thing to do.

My father could count and make himself understood in Italian, Spanish, French, and German. He did business and made deals with people who spoke all these languages.

At Kendall Hall, I had an Italian roommate whose father and mother were both born in Italy and spoke English with an accent. Mr. Mastrangelo had a window manufacturing business in Fitchburg. My father and Mr. Mastrangelo became good friends right away. It seemed so easy for them. I suppose counting in Italian helped. The simple approach to everything kept the way open and clear for bonds and friendships to develop easily.

They seem to operate on an uncomplicated gut level that allowed the chemistry to work.

He ran a very big business from our kitchen table with a telephone and a small black book. He would sit there every afternoon for two or three hours cutting deals for his super market business with vendors of meat, fish, poultry, and other saleable goods. He knew the prices of everything. He didn't need anything but his head to calculate the cost of goods by how many pounds he wanted. He seemed to have a table in his head that did all of that for him. He would write columns of numbers after he made the deal and know exactly what each item cost and how much he had to sell it for to make a profit. The deals were verbal agreements between buyer and seller, and never once was there an issue or argument. These men had respect for each other and the work they did. They also knew that if they broke that trust even once, business would be impossible to do.

Most of the men my father did business with were Jewish. He liked the Jews. He knew how to deal with them and they knew how to deal with my father.

I loved the straight talk my father used. He knew what he wanted and he knew how to get it. It was a game with its own set of rules. Everyone knew the rules and played the same game.

My father did business with a woman he always called "Miss Reba." She owned a wholesale fish business in Boston. The other dealers were men, and he called them either by their real name or, depending on how the deal was going, "stupid bastard" or "*gavone*" (Italian for stupid) or "*mishdoob*" (Arabic for stupid).

"Miss Reba, this is Louie, what are smelts going for today?"

"Oh, come on, I can get them for three cents from Hook."

"Okay, Miss Reba, let me know if you change your mind."

"Dad, you didn't talk to Hook about smelts," I would say, "How do you know what he wants for them?"

"Jackie, she knows I'm lying," he'd answer. "She wants to sell those fish as much as I want to buy them. She's lying, too, about the price. She knows it and I know it. But it works. She'll call back in a minute and we'll make the deal. Just wait."

And, of course, Miss Reba was right on time with the call and the deal. I loved watching and listening. He smoked one cigarette after the other all afternoon. He smoked Chesterfield cigarettes. I watched everything he did—how he lit the cigarette, blew out the match, rolled the ashes on the ashtray to get them off the tip, and sometimes hold the cigarette between his lips as he wrote in his book. I thought he looked great with the cigarette in his mouth and the smoke drifting up making him squint to see. His hands were strong, his fingers wide, but he could write more on a small piece of paper than anyone I have ever known. It seemed so easy and he was so organized.

He made little notes in his black book all afternoon and when he was finished, he called the manager of the meat department to give him the order, what to expect, and the prices. He must have been stressed at times, but I never saw it. He always seemed in control of the business part of his life.

I know the hard work was tough on him. He got up every morning before five o'clock and went into the wholesale markets in Boston. At the end of the day, his feet would ache. When I was home alone with him, he would ask me to get some hot water in his special small tub so that he could soak his feet. I was flattered that he would ask me to do anything for him. He usually waited for my mother to do things like that. He would sit for about twenty minutes with his feet in the water, and then ask me to dry them for him. I would do it, but was always afraid I was not doing it right. "That's good, Jackie You're doing a great job," he would say. He knew I was nervous. He never asked my brothers to help with his feet. Maybe he thought it was a girl's job.

My father had his first heart attack in September of my sophomore year in college. He wasn't supposed to drive after his heart attack. For the next two summers, he would ask me many times to drive him to Boston at the crack of dawn. He didn't talk very much, but when he did, he told stories that were almost like parables with one-line summaries, some of which I have never forgotten.

"It's OK to fight with people outside the family but never OK to fight with people inside the family."

"If you're an idiot and you go to college, you are a college bred idiot."

"People are no goddamned good."

We would go into the wholesale houses, where he introduced me to all of his friends. I felt very special with him.

"Your father is one tough SOB. He's the toughest guy in the market," one of his friends said.

"Don't listen to that old man, Jackie. He doesn't know what he's talking about," said father.

They all loved the chance to slap each other on the back. There was a warm camaraderie in the group that made everyone feel good.

During those two summers I drove my father, I met most of the wholesalers he knew. We always had coffee at the local coffee shop. It had sawdust on the floor, whirring fans overhead, and the smell of donuts frying in the new donut-making machine behind the counter.

In 1955 there was not much serious thought given to any man's daughter going into business with her father. That didn't keep men from teasing me and my father about a partnership for us in the future. It was always lightly delivered, but I held onto it inside with both arms.

During those two summers, I would also drive my father to Rockingham Race Track in Salem, New Hampshire on Wednesday afternoons. Wednesday was a sort of half day of work for my father and most of his wholesaler buddies. I was never sure what that was about, but it was midweek and maybe the needs of the businesses were slower. The same group of men that he haggled prices with in Boston would be in the clubhouse section of the race track. I didn't have a clue about odds or betting the "win, place, or show" up on the big board.

As the first summer wore on, I learned the whole scene. I was a runner for my father and anyone else in the group who wanted to place a bet at the window. I was nervous about getting the bet placed for the right horse at the right window and for the right slot for win, place, or show. I was also anxious because the rules were that you had to be twenty-one to bet on anything, and I was only nineteen that first summer. I always looked much older than I was and must have looked like I knew what I was doing. No one ever stopped me. In retrospect, there was no one my age or near it at the track. Most of the people there were my father's age or older, and they were so involved in the work of betting that they didn't notice anything or anyone.

Sometimes they won, and sometimes they lost. They always had fun and never seemed to care either way. The stakes were never high, mostly two-dollar bets. Win or lose, there was always a lot of back slapping and joking about who won or lost and why. Also, my father shared his winning tickets with me saying, "Buy something special for yourself." If his friends overheard this, they would start with the comments.

"Better take it while you can get it, Jackie. He's a tight SOB. He'll never offer it again."

"You're a lucky man, Louie, to have a daughter like Jackie,." one of the men would say,

"Jackie, when you graduate from school, come and see me, I'll have a good job for you."

We usually had something to eat, such as a hot dog and coke for me and a hot dog and beer for my father. The only time I ever saw him drink any kind of alcohol was at the track with his buddies and it was a beer. We left before the last race to avoid the big crush of traffic out of the parking lot.

"Do you want to drive, Dad?"

"No, Jackie, I want you to drive."

My father died when I was 21, the year I graduated from Connecticut College. My memories of him are more vivid today than they have ever been. It's curious how that should happen. I've fantasized about what life would have been like for me if my father had lived longer than age fifty four. I have whole chapters in my head about what life could have been if he had stayed with us.

Chapter 11

Adma Corey Ganem

My mother wanted everyone to love her. She worked very hard to be the best daughter-in-law to Sitho and the best sister-in-law to the women in the Big House when we lived there. I think she also believed she was being the best mother to the four of us. But, if she was going to be the best sister-in-law and the best daughter-in-law, then she couldn't be the best mother.

For example, Aunt Emma, my Uncle Kamel's wife, was only interested in being a good mother to her three children. That meant that she took care of them first, and no one else took care of them. If they needed discipline, she gave it to them, but no one else did. If she saw someone doing something she didn't like with her children, she told them so. She didn't seem to care at all if anyone liked her or not.

Aunt Betty, too, was always pleasant to everyone in the Big House, but she did whatever she wanted and didn't care what anyone thought about her. Aunt Julia was married to Uncle Bill, the oldest brother. This gave her some extra power in the group. It was only my mother who worked hard to please everyone. She tried very hard to have all of us do the same thing. Sometimes, it felt like we were on stage and my mother was the stage prompter. We were given long lists of "do's and don'ts" every day, such as:

"Be nice to everyone."

"Smile at everyone and say hello."

"Do what you are asked to do."

"Don't fight with your cousins."

My brother Billy once took a dollar from my mother's purse when he was in the second grade. He stopped at a candy store near school and bought all packages of bubble gum they had with baseball pictures. He only wanted the pictures, so at school he gave the gum away to his classmates. The teacher called my mother because it was so unusual for a second grader to have that much money to buy all that gum. My mother dropped everything and went to school to bring Billy home. She was embarrassed and humiliated that her son stole a dollar. There was a crazy kind of shock in the house about the crime. My mother punished Billy with a good hard spanking. Uncle Bill gave my mother a lecture on the seriousness of raising a thief and Billy a lecture on stealing.

There was a kind of double pressure on my mother. She came from the Corey family, who had been in partnership with the Ganems for several years before they split up and went into their own businesses. Gido Corey and Sitho Akaba were highly regarded by everyone in the community, just like the Ganems. My mother didn't want to disappoint anyone. The match between my father and mother was thought to be a very good one.

My mother did everything she was supposed to do and more. When we moved to Andover, she invited Aunt Julia and Uncle Bill for dinner about three times a week. She was the only sister-in-law to do that. She took Sitho out to shop once a week and, in grape-leaf season, she took Sitho to New Hampshire to pick the grape leaves so she could make stuffed rolled grape leaves. She worked very hard at always doing the right things. My mother was so busy doing all the things she thought she had to do that she hardly had time to love us. Oh, she made certain we took all kinds of lessons. We took dancing lessons, elocution lessons, fencing, piano, and violin. We went away to camp in the summer and private school in the winter. We had bicycles and nice clothes. But somehow, we were not as good or as accomplished or as smart as she wanted us to be. We grew up feeling like we had disappointed her. It was tough to be her, but it was even tougher being us. I remember feeling grateful having two brothers and a sister to share her attention with. My mother felt insecure and different, and she sometimes made us feel that same way.

I don't think my mother had an easy life. She worked hard to make life better, or what she thought was better. But it was always about her and no one else. She never stopped to think about us as separate from her. She couldn't see us—who we were or what we wanted. It made having a real relationship with her impossible.

When my father died, her world crumbled and she realized that the family she thought was hers was not. Not only was the family not hers, but they were, in fact, the enemy. My father's brothers took what was my mother's and ours and gave her only a small portion—what they decided was our share.

The shock of it all was so huge that for some time my mother didn't believe what was happening. The years she spent being dutiful, respectful, and the best sister-in-law came back and haunted her. The Big House became a reminder of all things tinged with disillusionment. She felt used, manipulated, tricked, and humiliated. When the shock subsided, she spent the rest of her life regretting the first part of her life and how she had lived it. She spent days sitting at the kitchen table reliving the past. She had conversations with everyone in the family in her head, conversations she wished she had and didn't have many years before. "What a fool I've been. What a mess I've made."

The regrets were many, too many to deal with. She began to drink too much. Nothing took away the pain of a lifetime misled.

I was home alone with my mother when our world changed. I saw her suffer but could do nothing about it. I had my own barriers up from years of needing to protect myself against not measuring up. At times I could feel nothing. I wanted to get away and escape. And I did escape, soon after, in a marriage that took me away from my mother, but in some ways into a relationship not unlike the one I left at home. Mother would say,

"I made so many mistakes with you. Can you ever forgive me?"

But many years later, when I told my mother I was getting a divorce she said,

"How can you do this to me? You've been married for twenty-five years, just stick it out. What will I say to everybody? What will I say if anyone asks about Bill? If anyone asks you, just tell them he's on a business trip."

"Do you hear what you're saying?" I answered. "I should stay in a marriage I don't want so you will feel okay? You don't care about me at all and you never have!"

It was the closest we had ever been to having an honest exchange that might have let us have a real relationship. It never happened, but she did listen. For the time left between the two of us, she looked at me and, for the first time, she saw me.

Chapter 12

Uncle Kamel

Uncle Kamel, one of my father's brothers, was the fourth son in the Ganem family. We laughed every time we said his name. When Sitho said his name, it sounded French, like Camille. He was a very odd-looking man. He was shorter than his brothers, maybe 5' 4" tall. He was bald and had large very poppy eyes. His wife, Emma, was taller than he was by three inches at least. She was blond, blue-eyed and quite attractive. She was English, which made her different from the rest of the family.

We all liked Uncle Kamel because he talked to us, told us jokes, and played card tricks for us. The other Uncles just said hello and patted us on the head. Uncle Kamel loved to play cards and do card tricks. He would rather be with the kids in the family than talking to his brothers about business. He only talked to them when he had to.

Emma and Kamel were the first family to move out of the Big House. Emma spent most of the day in her two rooms with her three children. She was respectful to Sitho and did the house chores she was assigned, but didn't socialize very much with the rest of the family. She was very happy to move away.

In 1938, they moved to Haverhill, Massachusetts, where Kamel was to manage one of the family markets. Aunt Margaret was sent to Haverhill to manage the office. It felt like a distant outpost. Kamel liked being away from his brothers. He and Margaret seemed to have a special bond. Margaret was always protective of Kamel. They were the two shortest people in the family and looked like they went together. If one of his brothers called to speak to Kamel and he was not in the market, Margaret would make up an excuse for him.

"He's out on the loading dock checking on a delivery."

"He went to the bank to make a deposit."

These were okay reasons to be away from the market. He was away more than he was there.

I don't know what kind of marriage Kamel and Emma had, but Emma loved her children and her house in Haverhill and always seemed content when she would visit the Big House on Sundays. She made English currant and lemon tarts to bring every Sunday. I loved the current tarts. I don't think Sitho ever ate one, but she would kiss Emma and thank her for the gift. Emma had learned just enough Arabic to understand Sitho and answer her in Arabic. Every once in a while on special holidays, Emma would bring her parents to the Big House. Mr. and Mrs. Pearson were very short, pale, and thin and very nice to everyone. They were quiet and sat together on the couch in the living room. The children in the family would parade up and say hello and offer to be kissed by Mrs. Pearson. There was a quiet contentment about them, which was very different from our family.

The Haverhill market opened in 1938 and closed in 1945. I remember that our Sunday visits around that time included some closed-door meetings with the brothers shouting and pounding on the table. Sometimes Uncle Kamel would come out and yell at Aunt Emma, "Get the kids! We're leaving!" Sitho never said anything when this would happen. Kamel would kiss her as he always did, and she would whisper her blessing in Arabic. Kamel had a whole other life away from the business. All the times Margaret made excuses for him not attending to the business, the word was he was away gambling.

"All the high rollers in New England must know that asshole!" my father said to my mother on one of our Sunday rides home from the Big House.

Everyone in the area knew about Kamel's gambling except his family. The bookkeeping was loose, and Margaret was there to cover up for Kamel. We heard that the money came in and the money went out. The family had to pay off some debt. Apparently, money was borrowed from some gangster types and they had threatened with blackmail and worse if it wasn't paid up.

Emma never changed through all of the tough times with Kamel and the family. She continued to make her currant and lemon tarts on Sundays. Margaret didn't change, either. Her brothers never asked her anything about the situation. Blanche and Margaret spent more and more time in their own rooms on those loud Sundays. The brothers calmed down and began to do some brain-storming about what to do with Kamel.

"We have to find a simple business for him, something we can watch," my father told my mother.

In 1947, the family bought a movie theater and a bowling alley in Lowell for Kamel to manage. Kamel and his family moved to Lowell and life quieted down for a while. When the theater opened, the whole family went for a private showing. We thought it was great fun to have a movie theater in our family. We had as much popcorn and candy as we wanted and could sit wherever we wanted. I can't remember the movie we saw. I must have been too busy moving around and eating. After the movie, we went to the bowling alley and bowled. We had to set up our own pins, but that was even more fun than bowling. I remember thinking how lucky our cousins Kenny, Bobby, and Elaine were to live near the movie theater and the bowling alley. They could go bowling every day after school and go the movies anytime they wanted—for free.

The beautiful time I imagined didn't last very long. Uncle Kamel died at age fifty in 1954. The dreams of great success that the family had for the fifty years they had been in this country were beginning to fade. At best, they had been stalled by family issues that were growing and by more complex times in the world that they didn't understand.

Chapter 13

Aunt Blanche and Aunt Margie

Aunt Blanche and Aunt Margie were their own team in the Big House. Aunt Blanche was the fifth child and first daughter in my father's family, and Aunt Margie was the sixth child. They were the only women in the family. Their brothers were respectful and courteous toward them, but never really talked to them, asked their advice, or even cared what they thought about anything. They had bedrooms on the third floor away from the other families.

They made an odd-looking couple. Aunt Margie was very short, maybe 4' 9". The story we heard was that Sitho didn't have enough time to feed Aunt Margie the right way and she didn't grow as she should have. She was not a pretty woman. She had a big nose and big ears, but she had an energy about her that made her likeable. She teased us sometime and seemed to like her nieces and nephews. We used Aunt Margie as a measure of how tall we were. Everyone was taller than Aunt Margie by the time we were nine or ten.

Aunt Blanche was 5' 4" tall. She was not a pretty woman either, but next to Aunt Margie, she was much better looking. My mother used to say that she could be a twin of Uncle John's. She shook her head like Uncle John and spoke the same way he did. It was a lot of sputtering and stuttering. My father called it "hocus-pocus." I think that meant they didn't want anyone to understand them anyway. She used the word "honey" all the time. Honey could be anyone, because she never used our names.

"Honey, do me a favor and get my coat."

"Honey, go tell Sitho what time it is."

Her piano playing was great. She could play anything and everything. We just had to hum a few notes and she could play the whole song. "She plays by ear," mother said.

It sounded very good to us however she played. Her head would jiggle back and forth in time with the music. Everyone clapped after each song.

Aunt Blanche and Aunt Margaret were best friends. They didn't socialize outside of the family. They worked in the family business and knew a lot of people, but when work was over they went home to the Big House and stayed there. They whispered and giggled together about the rest of the family. They gossiped all the time about everyone they knew. They gossiped about everyone in the family, too. They had favorites and let everyone know who they were. There was a cruel and thoughtless manner about them. It felt like they were getting even with everyone for the way they were treated by their brothers. Sitho was part of their group, but she was not mean. That group did not include the sisters-in-law, because they were connected to the brothers and did not share the same complaints.

When I look back at their behavior, I can understand how they must have felt like second-class members of the family. Their brothers made assumptions about them, such as they would do whatever their brothers asked; they would care for their mother, always; and, probably the worst one of all, Blanche and Margaret had no special needs or desires of their own, because they were without self. They were invisible to their brothers.

There was nothing sophisticated about Aunt Blanche and Aunt Margaret. It was not an intellectual decision they made to play favorites or to be cruel to those of us they didn't like. It felt more like animal instinct, a way to strike back.

At certain times of the year, Sitho used part of the third floor to dry special herbs, such as mint and zathar. It was a delicious smell that stayed on the third floor year round. My brother Billy loved the third floor. He liked to stand with his head over the railing looking down at the first floor hall and spit. It made a splat sound that he really liked. He would have to be careful not to spit when anyone was passing through. The other thing he liked about the third floor was the bathroom. Not exactly the bathroom itself, but some of the things that were in it. He especially liked the toothpaste called *Teel*. It was red and had a cinnamon flavor that he liked. He would taste it every chance he could, and take just a little so that no one knew any was missing. Aunt Margie and Aunt Blanche loved Billy. They never knew the things he did on the third floor. He always had a sweet smile on his face and it seemed that was all that mattered to them.

When we were still living in the Big House, sometimes Aunt Blanche and Aunt Margie would invite me and my two girl cousins, Elaine and Carol, up to the third floor to look at their jewelry. The boys were never included, even Billy. I never cared about the jewelry, but I did want to see their rooms and everything they had. We would never turn down the invitation, because that would be rude.

The rooms were big and had big walk-in closets that smelled like cedar. Cedar and perfume filled both of the rooms, and the furniture was almost the same. It was dark mahogany and very big. They each had a dressing table with a big mirror and lots of drawers where they kept their jewelry. The rugs were oriental.

Elaine liked the jewelry more than Carol or me. We would stand around the dressing table while Aunt Blanche brought out each piece with a story about where it came from and how precious it was. We couldn't touch the really expensive pieces. Aunt Blanche would hold them and sometimes put them on to show us their beauty. She had lots of pins: pins with stones, pins in the shape of bows, and gold pins with religious-looking figures on them. There were more religious things than anything else.

"Now look at these beautiful statues," she would say, "This one can help you find something if it's lost; this one will keep you safe when you travel; and this one . . . this one can help you find a husband! You should each have one of these," she giggled."

"I don't want one," I said, "I don't want a husband."

"I'll take it," Elaine was quick to say.

"Me too," Carol said.

"I can't give this to you yet, I have to find a husband first, And, you, Jackie, of course you want a husband, what would you do without one?" Aunt Blanche would say, giggling again.

We would check out Aunt Margie's jewelry, too. This was a little easier than looking at Aunt Blanche's. Aunt Margie didn't have a lot of saints or crucifixes. She had lots of beads. She wore them all the time, and they made a jingling sound as she walked. We each got beads and a globe from the 1939 World's Fair in New York. Aunt Margie was more generous than Aunt Blanche. We would put the beads around our necks and jingle down two flights of stairs moving back and forth fast to make the beads jingle louder.

As she said she would, Aunt Blanche kept the saint to help her find a husband, and she did find one. His name was Ted Syak and he owned a restaurant in Stoneham. I think my Uncle Bill found Ted. It must have been arranged by both families, because they didn't date each other very long before getting married. They visited each other's families and relatives, and that was it. Ted and Blanche didn't know each other, they just knew each other's families. They were both Lebanese, they were both Catholic, Ted had a business, and Blanche's family had a business. That was enough to make a marriage.

We all went to the Ted's restaurant to see it and try it out. It was called "Ted's Inn." Next to the restaurant there were pony rides that Ted owned, too. This seemed to us to be a great marriage that would allow us free food and free pony rides anytime we wanted. Ted's sister, Vickie, worked in the restaurant. She seemed to do everything—wait on tables, cook, and collect the money. The restaurant was plain but nice inside, sort of like the old Howard Johnson restaurants. It had a bar with stools and also booths for regular dining. We went there a few times during the courtship and it was never busy.

Vickie had jet black hair that looked like doll's hair. It was pulled tightly into a bun and always had a pencil sticking out of it in the back. Her face always looked freshly washed and shiny with no makeup. She wore a uniform with a small, white apron and a little white hat that stood up like a crown.

She lived with Ted in a brick house not far from the restaurant. They did not have a big family like ours; there were just the two of them. I guessed that Vickie was not at all like Aunt Blanche. She probably didn't have a lot of jewelry. When Ted was around, he was very nice to Vickie. It was clear that he liked her.

Each time we went to "Ted's Inn," Vickie brought out special food for us. things that were not on the menu.

"Try this, *ya binthe*(my dear), I made it fresh today."

"Honey, would you like a coke?" (She called us honey a lot like Aunt Blanche did, but she didn't know our names.)

We never paid for anything when we went there, not even the pony rides. Vickie wouldn't take any money. "We're family now," she'd say.

Ted didn't work in the restaurant. He didn't seem to work anywhere.

"He's a deal maker," Uncle Bill told my father.

"Deal maker? What kind of deals? What has he done? What kind of work is that anyway?" My father had his doubts.

Aunt Blanche got married at a very small ceremony with only the main members of her family present. Aunt Margie was the maid of honor and Uncle Bill gave Aunt Blanche away.

"Uncle Bill really doesn't like Aunt Blanche at all to give her away," I said to my father. He laughed.

"Will she come back to the Big House at all? Aunt Margie is going to miss her."

I was actually thinking about the dresser in her room and how maybe Carol and

Elaine and I could look at everything alone without Aunt Blanche. Then we could try things on and take what we wanted.

We could tell that Sitho and Aunt Margie missed Aunt Blanche. Aunt Blanche and Ted went to New York City and then to Bermuda on their honeymoon. Aunt Margie couldn't even talk to her on the phone while she was away.

Well, Aunt Margie didn't miss her for long. When Ted and Aunt Blanche came home from their honeymoon, Aunt Blanche spent one night in Ted's brick house with Vicki and then came home to the Big House and back to her room on the third floor. The third floor wouldn't have been the same without Aunt Blanche, and who would play the piano on Sundays?

There was a lot of talk about Ted and the marriage. Mostly, people whispered about it. My mother and her sisters-in-law wondered.

"Did she decide she didn't like Ted?"

"Maybe she didn't like the sex."

"Was Vickie mean to her?"

"Was Blanche going to have to work in the restaurant and not be the bookkeeper in Ganem's market in Lawrence?"

"That was some lousy saint statue she had. She found a husband, but didn't keep him," I said to Carol and Elaine.

We laughed and I reconfirmed my view about not wanting a husband anyway. Aunt Blanche kept the diamond ring from Ted. She would take it out and show it to us when we went to look at her jewelry. She never wore it, but kept it in a very special place in her dressing table.

A decision was made to have the marriage annulled. Father David from the Lebanese church helped. He was a close family friend and Uncle Bill was head of the board at the church and the major contributor. A little extra money to Father David and the annulment was done. Aunt Blanche always went to church every Sunday, but after the marriage, she began to go every day.

Aunt Blanche was happiest in the Big House, working in the office of Ganem's market in Lawrence, and playing the piano on Sundays for our family talent shows. She jiggled her head as she played and giggled a little more than before she was married. The funny thing was, she kept Ted's last name as her own. She had checks that said Blanche Ganem Syak. She didn't want anyone to forget that she had been married.

She loved being in the office and being the boss of the office people. Most of the people who worked for the business were from the Lebanese community and grateful to have a job. They did whatever Blanche told them to do without complaining. Blanche was in charge of the money in the office. She spent most of her day counting the money and putting little wrappers around the piles. She wore little rubber fingers on her hands to help with the counting. I loved those little fingers and asked her for them every chance I had. They were treasures. There were piles of ones, fives, tens, and twenties in bundles of $100.00 stacked on her desk that overlooked the main floor of the market. The offices were in a mezzanine with all glass walls looking down at the sales floor.

On occasional Wednesdays, my mother would drive my father to work so that she could have the car and my father would take a half-day off. The half day wasn't really a half day. He went to Boston no later than 5:00 a.m. to buy the meats and other goods. Then he spent time in the office and in the meat-cutting room, so that by three o'clock in the afternoon he had put in a full day. My mother would meet him in his office, but would visit with Aunt Blanche for a while.

"Blanche is such a whiz in the office," she would tell my father.

"She can count that money and carry on a conversation with me at the same time."

That was not true about Aunt Blanche's accuracy. Most days, the bank would call with errors and corrections that had to be made to the deposits. One of the office workers would have to go to the bank to fix things up, and Aunt Blanche swore the helper to secrecy. "Don't tell anyone about this. Let's keep it between the two of us."

The office help all knew that Blanche made mistakes every day, and it was part of their job to fix things up. Even her brothers thought that Blanche knew what she was doing. They suspected she was taking money for herself from the business. When the business was growing and doing well, no one seemed to care. There was enough to go around. She never took a day off. She worked six days a week. If the market was open for business, Aunt Blanche was there. The problem was that Blanche began to think that the business was hers and it wasn't.

When we were a little older, we were allowed to go to the market in Lawrence on Saturdays to help out. Mid-morning, my mother would drop off Billy, Allan, and me for two or three hours. Aunt Blanche was in charge of assigning us to work. Allan would sweep the office. Billy was the oldest, so he would get to go into the meat lockers to do whatever the butchers asked him to do. He smelled like meat and had rosy cheeks and cold hands at the end of the day. He usually had some stories to tell about what went on in the locker. Aunt Blanche sent me out to ask all of the clerks if they needed any change.

Billy loved what he did.

"I cut some hens open and there were real eggs inside," he'd say.

"You're fooling me, I don't believe it. Next time you see that, come and get me, I want to see it, too," I'd answer.

I was out and about and could sneak into the meat locker. Poor Allan was stuck with Aunt Blanche in the office.

Aunt Blanche had a big basket on a rope that she could lower through a sliding glass door down to the sales floor. I would check with the clerks and, if they needed change, they would give me the money and ask for a roll of quarters or dimes or sometimes one-dollar bills. I would then walk back, call up to Aunt Blanche with the request, and she would lower the basket for the money and then return it with the change.

I liked the job. Everyone was nice to me, and I could take whatever I wanted to eat anytime I felt like it. I loved the donut-making machine and the donuts it made. Dough was dropped into hot oil and half way around the circular machine the donuts would be flipped over to cook on the other side. At the end of the circle, the donuts were flipped out, hot and ready to be dipped in sugar, cinnamon, or frosting. I usually had at least one donut every time I worked.

"Don't eat all the profits," the donut lady would say. I didn't know what that meant, but I would smile and say, "Oh, I won't."

My mother would come back to pick us up and Aunt Blanche would pay us for our work. She would hand us each a small, sealed manila envelope with our names on it. "I hope they weren't too much trouble," my mother always said.

"Oh no, honey, no trouble at all."

When we left the office we ripped open our envelopes. It always meant trouble. Aunt Blanche never gave us the same amount of money. Billy always got more than Allan or me, and Allan always got the smallest amount. Aunt Blanche loved Billy and didn't like Allan. I was a girl so it didn't matter what she gave me. I was lucky to get anything at all, I guessed. Allan always wanted to go back to Aunt Blanche and tell her how mean she was and how unfair and how much he hated her. My mother wouldn't let him go. She never wanted to cause trouble. She gave Allan more money to even things out with Billy. Aunt Blanche liked to cause trouble.

Allan was a tricky guy. If he didn't like something, he said so. That may not sound too tricky, but in the Big House it was. Allan was the only one who spoke up about anything. The rest of us just did what we were supposed to do. Or even if we didn't, we never said anything; we smiled all the time and said, "yes", and "please" and "thank you."

Many years later, when Allan was a grown young man, Allan had a run-in with Aunt Blanche. Aunt Blanche was still working in the office counting money, only then she was in the Lynn market. Allan and Billy were working there, really running the place. On this particular day, Allan noticed that one of the employees was following him around the store. His name was Ray Mancinelli. Mid day, Allan confronted him.

"Ray, what's going on? Are you following me?"

"Oh, Al, I didn't want to do it, but Blanche told me to watch you and let her know everything you were doing."

Allan went into a rage that brought up all the hurts he had endured through the years in the Big House, especially from Aunt Blanche. He stormed up to the office, opened the door, and slammed it shut. Blanche looked startled and afraid.

"What the fuck do you think you're doing, spying on me? This is not your business! Pack up your stuff and get the fuck out, now. This business is mine, not yours. Who do you think you are? *Now*, Blanche, *right now*. Do you hear me?"

Blanche was speechless. She muttered and shook. She moved stuff around on the desk.

'Honey, please, I'm sorry, don't tell anyone, don't tell your mother."

"Shut the fuck up and get out!"

There was no more close family.

The last time I saw Aunt Blanche was in 1970, shortly before she died. Blanche was not well, and my mother thought we should pay her a visit. She was living in a small house in Andover, having moved there from Marblehead where she lived with Sitho and Aunt Margie before they had passed away. My mother called to tell Blanche that we would stop in on Friday evening. She was waiting for us.

Aunt Blanche had put all of the furniture from the bigger house in Marblehead into the small Andover house. The living room had two couches, four large chairs, and huge lamps on four big tables. The floor had an oriental rug that had to be folded on the sides because it was too big for the room. In the middle of the room was the baby grand piano from the Big House. It was difficult to move in the room. The dining room was not much better. The table was too long for the room and jutted out into the living room.

There were twelve chairs, mostly lining the walls of the room.

Aunt Blanche had stopped going to the beauty parlor for hair cuts and color; she did it all herself. Her hair was various shades of gray, brown, and black. It depended on when you saw her just what color would be predominant. When we saw her, it seemed equally colored one third of each shade. She had rollers in her hair, as if she had plans to go out and was preparing herself. She had dressed up in a dress that my mother thought was her going away dress when she married Ted. I couldn't tell; they all looked the same to me, like house dresses that were too big.

There was a sense of entering another world as we dodged our way through the furniture in the living room. She was happy to see us, but seemed more nervous than usual. She still had the little jiggle of her head and sputtering speech. She led us into the dining room where she had set the table for us. We were not eating dinner with her, but she had a table full of snacks that she had laid out hours before. The cheese and crackers were curling at the edges, the vegetable platter was wilted, the Syrian bread was hard and the *baba ghanoush* (eggplant spread) had a crust on it. We

59

spent about an hour with her and managed to eat a couple of her snacks, washing them down with soda she served.

She asked about everyone in our family. Her world had not grown beyond the Ganem family, and that's how she had always been. If she was uncomfortable with family, it would have been too difficult for her to be with strangers; in her world, there were only family and strangers anyway.

About a year later, Aunt Blanche died. She left everything she had to her favorite brother, Emil, along with all the furniture. She left small amounts of money to favorite nephews. She left money to my brother Billy and nothing to the rest of us. Billy divided the money with us to make things fair. Aunt Blanche just couldn't do that.

Chapter 14

Uncle Bill and Aunt Julia

Uncle Bill was the oldest in the family, which meant that he was the most important and was treated with extra respect by everyone. Even Sitho and Gido gave Uncle Bill special attention. Although the family business name was "Joseph Ganem and Sons," everyone knew that it should have read, "William J. Ganem and Brothers."

Uncle Bill was also different because he and Aunt Julia didn't have any children. Aunt Julia had two babies, but they both died. In their bedroom there was a big picture of one of the babies. When I was in their bedroom I would take a quick glance at the picture. I felt like I wasn't supposed to do that.

Aunt Julia made certain that no one ever forgot how important Uncle Bill was. Almost every day, if Uncle Bill was around, she would say to one of us, "Who's the most wonderful man in the world?" or "Who's the smartest man in the world?"

We knew the answer and, in chorus, we would say, "Uncle Bill."

Uncle Bill would smile and show his two gold teeth. He's the only one in the family that had gold teeth. Then Aunt Julia would tell us to kiss Uncle Bill.

Uncle Bill had an office in the Lawrence market. It was the biggest office with the best view of the first Ganem's Market. My father and Uncle Kamel were too busy to sit down at all. Uncle John had his law office and Uncle Emil was still in medical school. Uncle Bill would do some buying in the morning, but in the afternoon he would sit and look out over the market. His office was on a mezzanine above the store floor with all glass windows. Some afternoons Aunt Julia would come to town, stop and have lunch at the Puritan Tea Room, and then spend the rest of the afternoon with Uncle Bill in his office.

He was a leader in the Lebanese community, so he would often have visitors coming to ask his advice or counsel on private or community business. Father David was a frequent visitor. Aunt Julia would ask one of the clerks in the office to go down and get some fruit or cookies to serve to the guests.

Everyone listened to Uncle Bill, but not everyone did what he told them to do. Aunt Blanche, for example, was always respectful in front of him. She would say, "Yes, Bill," or "Of course, Bill," or "Whatever you say, Bill." But then she would go back to her office and get on the phone with her sister, Aunt Margie, and giggle, jiggle her head and say something in Arabic as she'd glance in the direction of Uncle Bill's office. Uncle Bill smoked cigars and Aunt Julia smoked cigarettes, so the office was always full of smoke. Sometimes from the floor of the market you couldn't make out who was in the office. When the door opened, the smoke escaped into the hall. The whole office area smelled of smoke.

I loved to watch Uncle Bill when he smoked. His hands were white and his fingers had black hairs on them. His fingernails were neatly clipped. He would unwrap the cigar and then clip off the end with a special clipper he had in his vest pocket. He would roll the cigar in his mouth to get it wet. He did this for a long time. Then he lit the cigar, puffing many times with the flame of the wooden match flaring each time he puffed.

We never talked to Uncle Bill and he didn't talk to us. The communicating was done through Aunt Julia. The only one of the children who ever talked to Uncle Bill was my brother Allan. Allan didn't like Uncle Bill, and Uncle Bill didn't like Allan. Even when Allan was three years old, it was clear to everyone that he didn't like Uncle Bill.

None of us believed that Uncle Bill was that special, but we knew what was expected of us. Allan was the only one who dared not respond as expected to the question about who was the best man in the world. He answered, "I don't think Uncle Bill is the best man in the world. I think my father is."

My mother would wince and her teeth would clench. If she was near Allan she would pinch him on his arm. If she wasn't close enough to pinch, she would open her eyes wide and mouth the answer, "Uncle Bill," hoping Allan would see her and say it. This never happened. Allan was strong, and he liked the trouble he caused with Uncle Bill. From then on,

Uncle Bill was focused on Allan. He waited for any little waiver from what was expected and pounced on him.

There was no way Uncle Bill was going to win anything with Allan. My mother knew, as a mother does, that Allan was a tough character and that nothing would make him retract or change. We all knew this about Allan, except Uncle Bill. Here was a grown man locked in battle with a three year old, and he was not going to win. Because

Uncle Bill believed what Julia said about him, that he was the smartest and best man in the world, giving in to this three-year-old just wasn't possible.

Just before we moved out of the Big House, Uncle Bill and Allan did battle over a lunch that Allan would not eat. Allan was a picky eater. Even Sitho made special things for him to eat. Uncle Bill stayed home from work that afternoon "to teach Allan a lesson." We all stayed close enough to watch. They sat at the table in front of a dish of imjaddarah (lentils) all afternoon. Allan did some fidgeting, but never put the spoon to his mouth. Uncle Bill scowled and put the spoon to Allan's lips, but his lips were sealed shut; he could stay that way for a long time. The rest of us peeked around corners from the living room. We knew Allan would win and he did, but then he had to go to his room for the rest of the day.

We secretly thought Allan was very brave. These were tough times for my mother. The whole thing embarrassed her. She knew that Allan wouldn't give in, but she never had the courage to speak up and defend him. She was afraid of Uncle Bill, and I think that she bought into the "Bill is the smartest and greatest" business.

My father was never around for these events. I have often wondered what my father would have done if he had been there with Allan and Uncle Bill. I hoped that he would defend Allan and not just let him be bullied by Uncle Bill, but I'm not sure that would have happened.

Uncle Bill was a bully with everyone in his family. His brothers bought into the whole thing that Julia promoted with us. When the business was just beginning to flourish, Bill was the leader, the man with the biggest desk and the biggest office. Bill would say, "Trust me" and everyone did. Aunt Julia made it her main mission to promote Bill to himself and to the whole family. The family let it go, because they didn't have any children.

Bill and Julia had the best bedroom in the house; better even than my Sitho and Gido. It was in the front of the house, it was the biggest and brightest, and it had four very large windows. It was also decorated very differently than the rest of the house. It was very dressy looking. We never went in there unless we were invited, which wasn't very often. The windows had many layers of curtains—some were draped and some were straight and filmy. There was lace all over everything. The overall color was pink. The furniture was off-white with gold trim, and everything matched. The lamps were large with square shades that had little pink balls dangling all around. There was a picture of their baby, Edward, on the wall and a large portrait of Julia sitting on a bench with a big floppy hat on her lap.

Two pieces of furniture were unique to their room; no one else had anything like them. One was a white satin chaise lounge with a few small, pink pillows. The other piece was a dressing table with a big ornate mirror and a chair that looked like a queen's throne in front of it.

Once in a while, Julia would show her room to visitors, and you would hear great "oohs and aahs" coming from the guests. It was that special. Julia would beam.

On a few occasions, Aunt Julia invited me into her room when she was putting makeup on her face. I could sit on the chaise lounge, but not lie on it. I loved watching her. My mother never put makeup on like Julia. No one did. It was a lot of work and no one else had the time.

Aunt Julia would seat herself on her queen-like chair and put a cape around her neck. She never dropped or spilled anything, so I never could understand the need for the cape, but it was part of the ritual. She didn't just put it on, she would stroke the front of it several times to smooth it out and make a few more adjustments before she continued. She would light a cigarette with a pink table lighter and take a deep, loud breath and blow the smoke out in front of her. She put the cigarette in an ashtray on her dressing table and began with two kinds of creams. One went on and then got wiped off. The next one went on and stayed on, followed by a layer of powder. There were four or five of everything on the table in front of her, but she knew just which one to pick for each layer. She would stop to take a puff on the cigarette and to look closely in the mirror between each item. She usually put a dark red rouge all over her cheeks and moved it around with her fingers. Then she would take another puff of her cigarette. She then took a scissors-like thing and curled her eyelashes. It looked like it must hurt, but she kept it on there for a few minutes, so I guess it didn't bother her. She would put some blackish cream under her eyebrows, take two more puffs of the cigarette, and light another one.

She was coming close to the end now. She closed her lips and put some more powder on her face. She put lipstick on once, blotted it with a tissue, and put it on again. Finally, she looked in the mirror very closely and made a humming type noise. The cape came off, and that was it. Her lipstick always looked like it was on crooked, but maybe her lips were crooked. She finished up with a few squirts of perfume. Now the room smelled of smoke, perfume, and powders. I liked the smell.

In 1946, Uncle Bill had a stroke. He lost his speech and the use of his right side for sometime. He was at the Phillips House at the Massachusetts General Hospital. Slowly, his speech came back, but he was slow and seemed very different to all of us—but no one talked about it. His doctor recommended a special new treatment called "the rice diet," which was developed in 1934 at Duke University's department of medicine by Dr. Walter Kempner, specifically for people with various health problems, including stroke. The diet was all rice and very little else. Uncle Bill and Aunt Julia went to Duke from then on twice a year for two weeks at a time to have tests and adjustments made to the diet.

Uncle Bill began to sneak other food behind Aunt Julia's back. Who could blame him? Even after a few months, the only additional things he could eat were special things made of rice, for example, rice cookies, rice cakes, rice cereal, and rice muffins. When Aunt Julia wasn't around and Uncle Bill returned to his perch in the office, he would send whoever was around to get him some real cookies, some fresh fruit; anything he wanted. He would eat all day, hide food in his desk, and even smoke a cigar. He continued to drive, but he had accidents all the time. He backed up without looking, and scraped the car many times getting into and out of the garage.

The first summer after his stroke, my father thought it would be relaxing for Uncle Bill and Aunt Julia to spend the summer with us on Corbett's Pond in southern New Hampshire where we had a cottage. My mother was not happy, but had no choice. Uncle Bill spent the summer sitting on the deck watching us swim, boat, fish, water ski, and fight. My mother spent the summer cooking for Aunt Julia and Uncle Bill and us to working hard to keep Uncle Bill away from Allan. Uncle Bill would offer to drive get gas for the out board motor. My mother was so distracted she never thought about what kind of experience that might be for all of us. Uncle Bill had never been a good driver, but after the stroke he was frightening.

Our cottage was down a narrow dirt road, which was lined by trees and, in some places with water. We chose to sit in the back seat, ducking as we swerved by the trees. Uncle Bill scraped both sides of the car as we swung side to side. We once got stuck on a bank by the water with the rear wheels up in the air. Uncle Bill called one of the truck drivers from the market to get us out. We were desperate for the gas.

Only once did Uncle Bill ask to go out in the boat with us. We had a talk and fight about who would drive and who would sit next to Uncle Bill on the ride. Allan decided not to go. The boat was tied to the end of the dock, but the water was not deep there, maybe four feet. We tried to tell Uncle Bill how to get into the boat, but he either couldn't listen or didn't want to listen. He put one foot in the boat and had the other one on the dock, the boat moved out, and Uncle Bill did a split into the water. Allan was laughing. Billy and I were trying not to laugh and feeling a little panicky about Uncle Bill, who flailed his arms, lost his glasses, and sputtered and spit the water out of his mouth. He looked helpless and childlike. Aunt Julia flew out of the cottage and helped us get Uncle Bill on the beach. She spoke to him like a child and he answered like a child.

It could have been easy to feel sorry for Uncle Bill, but we didn't feel sympathy for him, because he was not as innocent as he looked in 1946. Before his stroke, he had bought several pieces of property for himself from family money. He also bought two businesses, one for himself and one for the family. My father resisted believing that his favorite brother would do this. He was convinced that Uncle John must have been behind the deceit. It was only after he and my mother went to check the Registry of Deeds that he was convinced.

Uncle Bill died in 1948 before there was any resolution between my father and him. Bill had always been the backbone of the family business. He was respected and trusted. I know it broke my father's heart to know that his brother had betrayed him. My father was like a little boy with his family. He believed in the myth of the family. He was the only one that did.

Chapter 15

Uncle John and Aunt Betty

Uncle John was two years older than my father. He was a lawyer. No one, not even my father, could understand how he became a lawyer. He just wasn't very smart.

"He doesn't know his ass from a hole in the ground," father said every time his name came up.

"He must have paid someone for the answers to the bar or had that thieving friend of his, Tommy Lane, pull some strings."

Uncle John was taller than his brothers, maybe 5' 6". He was slick in the way he dressed, and he wore his hair greased straight back with lots of Vaseline. He wore pinstripe suits with vests and stiff white shirts. He also wore spats and a gray fedora hat with a black hatband. He had a gold watch on a heavy gold chain that hung on his vest in a special watch pocket. He was not a good-looking man, appearing nervous and jerky when he moved, but people did turn to look at him. He had a big nose and big ears with black fuzzy hair around his ears and coming out of his nose. His clothes said, "Look at me. I'm important." He was the only one in the family who dressed that way.

He shared an office with his friend, Thomas J. Lane, who was a United States Representative from Essex County. Their office was on the top floor of the Craig building in Lawrence. The Craig building and the Bay State building were the two best office buildings in the city. The office door read: Thomas J. Lane, A. John Ganem, Attorneys at Law.

My Father used to say, "A. John Ganem, what is that shit anyway? His name is Aziz John, not A. John." It didn't matter that father had changed his name from Elias Louis to E. Louis. He didn't like much about his brother John.

We thought the change to A. John was neat. It sounded very fancy, like something you would see in the movies. My brother Billy talked about changing his name to W. Louis, and my brother Allan was going to change his to A. Joseph. I wanted to change my name too, but girls didn't do that. Anyway, J. Louise didn't sound right.

Everyone called Thomas Lane "Tommy," and he had served time in prison for some infraction of the law. No one seemed to mind. He even got re-elected after his prison term. Everyone liked Tommy. He had a bushy head of white hair that always looked like it needed to be combed. He had red cheeks and a reddish nose and smiled all the time. He knew everyone in the city and spoke to everyone. The office was always filled with people waiting to see Tommy. Uncle John didn't have many clients except family members and one or two Lebanese people from the city. Tommy didn't dress like Uncle John. His suits were always rumpled looking, he didn't wear a vest or spats, and his shoes were scuffed.

Everything about Uncle John was different from the other men in the family. He didn't work as much as anyone else. He left late in the morning and came home early. We saw more of Uncle John than any other man in the Big House.

There was a tile bathroom off the kitchen that all of the children in the family used. The only adult that used the bathroom was Uncle John. Every morning he shaved in that bathroom. He had a long leather strap that he sharpened his straight razor on before he shaved. He never shut the door to the bathroom and popped in and out first with his shaving mug and brush twirling in his hand, then out again with soap all over his face then after two or three swipes with the razor and so on until he finished the job and wiped the rest of the soap off his face. He had to see what was going on.

Every morning there were six or seven of us in the kitchen playing. Some of us were waiting to go to school and some of us weren't yet in school. Playing meant pushing and shoving, talking and laughing, and sometimes crying. Uncle John never did understand any of that, especially after he had Carol, his oldest child.

"OK, who hit Carol?" he would say.

"No one, Uncle John," two or three voices would answer.

"Who hit you, honey?" Uncle John would ask Carol. Carol was too young to talk and would just cry and point to anyone.

"What hand did you do it with?" he'd ask. Guilty or not made no difference; someone had to pay. No one answered. Uncle John would decide who and with what hand and take the same ear and twist it, hard. We were glad to see Uncle John go to work.

Uncle John was married to Aunt Betty who was from Montreal, Canada. I never understood why Sitho, Gido, Aunt Julia, and Uncle Bill went to Canada to find a wife for Uncle John. There was a large Lebanese community in Lawrence with many eligible young women. But John was a lawyer and maybe that meant something special like going out of the country for a wife. John was proud to have Betty for his wife. She was young, had beautiful red hair, a pretty face, and she looked grand on his arm.

I loved Aunt Betty; most people did. She was very energetic and full of fun. Aunt Betty's family was very happy about the arrangement. Uncle John was from a good family and he was a lawyer. Sitho Tabah (Aunt Betty's mother) was just like Aunt Betty. She was fun and lively. We loved the times that Sitho Tabah visited the Big House. It meant fun and games. Our own Sitho was wonderful to us, but she never had time to play. None of the Ganems had time to play or have fun.

Aunt Betty didn't know Uncle John at all before she married him, and it became clear very soon that she was surprised at who he was.

"What's all the noise about in here?" Uncle John would say as he came out of the bathroom with his razor in his hand and soap all over his face.

"We're playing London Bridges, John," Aunt Betty would say. Aunt Betty was on her hands and knees going under the bridge that Billy and Allan made for her. Uncle John jiggled his head, sputtered something no one could understand, and went back into the bathroom.

"He might pull your ear, Aunt Betty," Allan said. "He does that to us when we make too much noise."

"Don't worry, honey, he won't pull my ear. No siree, Bobalu ayé!" She talked like that all the time.

Sitho came out of the pantry to see what was happening. She didn't say anything and went back to her cooking. She liked Aunt Betty, too, in the beginning. We could hear her talking in the pantry in Arabic to Aunt Julia. In the middle of the Arabic we heard, "Bobalu ayé." Sitho didn't know that language and neither did we, but we were all going to hear more of it and understand it as the days passed.

Aunt Betty changed after Carol was born. She was still fun and played with all of us when she had the time, but she wasn't content to stay in the Big House with the other wives. She did what she wanted to do. She got a babysitter for Carol and called a taxi to take her out. She never told anyone where she was going or when she would be back, not even Uncle John. She became the main topic of conversation in the house. Sitho didn't talk to her daughters-in-law about Betty, but she did talk to Aunt Blanche and Aunt Margie.

Aunt Betty didn't change. She still played with all of us. She sang songs, and she was smiling and pleasant to everyone. She did what she was supposed to do, but she also did what she wanted to. She also began going out at night. At first, she went out only when Uncle John had to work late, but then she just went out anytime she felt like it.

Aunt Julia was the biggest gossip in the group. She loved the drama of it, Aunt Betty's activity excited her. She reported everything she knew and heard to Uncle Bill, the oldest in the family and the boss of everyone.

"Did you hear about how she came home last night?" Aunt Julia would say,

"She had too much to drink, can you imagine that? She has the nerve to come down here every morning like nothing's happened."

Of course, no one could imagine that. The Ganems didn't drink anything alcoholic, ever. Uncle Bill talked to Uncle John to tell him to do something about Betty. "We have a reputation to maintain, for God's sake, Aziz, put a stop to this." Uncle Bill called Uncle John Aziz when he was mad at his brother.

Nothing John did or said to Aunt Betty made any difference to her. She went on doing whatever she wanted, keeping her own schedule.

There was a gossip newspaper in Lawrence called *The Tattler*, and they knew all there was to know in the city. Aunt Betty's activities became the main attraction in the paper.

"What wife of a prominent lawyer was seen at the Capri at closing?" read one of the bylines.

The Ganems were humiliated by the article. Uncle Bill was in a rage at Aziz. The Big House was blanketed in a quietness; even we were not as noisy as usual and, when we were, we were hushed by everyone with the "shh" of fingers to the lips.

Uncle John was a nervous wreck. He muttered and mumbled and jiggled his head. Uncle Bill told him to call Aunt Betty's mother, Sitho Tabah and see if she could stop her wild behavior.

Sitho Tabah was just like Aunt Betty. She was fun and had tricks for us that we had never seen before. She made a mouse from a handkerchief and she could make it jump. It scared us at first but we learned to like it. She also taught us the *dubke*, a Lebanese group dance that she led us in with the same mouse handkerchief. We didn't have music to dance to, but she sang the dubke song, "Ticki, ticki, tum, tum, tum." She clapped her hands and led us around.

Sitho Tabah had a wonderful visit at the Big House. Aunt Betty and Sitho Tabah went out most afternoons shopping and stopping for a snack at the Puritan Tea Room on Essex Street, just a block away from the Craig Building. After a two-week stay, she left and nothing changed. Sitho Ganem and Sitho Tabah had known each other for a very long time. Although they were very different people, they had a respect for each other. As the problems with Aunt Betty grew and Sitho Tabah could not or would not help, the relationship between the two women became strained.

"We had to pay *The Tattler* off to keep the stories out of the paper," My father told my mother. "My brother is an asshole, period. He always was and always will be."

Through all of this action in the house, Aunt Betty never changed, except that her hair became more and more red. She kept her happy face and continued to play with us. She was the only adult in the house that paid any attention to us. She had a sweet and loving way.

"Come here sweetheart; let me tie your shoes."

"How pretty you look today, *halween hal wich*." (How pretty your face.) Aunt Betty had two more babies, Joey and Ginger. They were sweet little babies. Joey had black hair and white skin. Ginger had reddish hair like Aunt Betty. There were more and more whispers in the house. Everyone seemed to care more about Aunt Betty and her mysterious ways than Uncle John did. He loved his new little babies. Who knows what he thought, if anything. He just jiggled his head a little more and continued to talk so no one understood him.

Uncle John and his family moved out of the Big House soon after Ginger was born in 1946. They settled into a house on Birchwood Road. Aunt Betty's life didn't change and Uncle John never did anything about it. Everyone knew her; she liked a good time. There were those who whispered behind her back and did the disapproving "tsk, tsk," with their tongues, but most people who knew Betty liked her. Furthermore, people who knew both Aunt Betty and Uncle John understood why Aunt Betty went out looking for a good time.

"She's not satisfied at home."

"What's wrong with John that he can't satisfy his own wife."

Uncle John never did anything to stop Aunt Betty. Life was easier for him away from the Big House. His brothers stopped advising him. He kept Aunt Betty out of trouble. He never got mad at her. We think he was afraid she would leave him.

Over time, most of us had our own Aunt Betty stories. My cousin Bobby literally bumped into Aunt Betty coming out of the Manger Hotel next to North Station. He was on his way home from college. Aunt Betty had no money and needed to get home.

"Honey, can you help me out. I lost my pocketbook somewhere and I have no money to get home." Her lipstick was smudged and she had a run in her stocking.

"Please, sweetheart."

Bobby took Aunt Betty's arm and led her to a bench in the station.

"Sit here, Aunt Betty, I'll help you." Bobby wasn't sure if she had been drinking or she was just confused.

He bought her a ticket to Lawrence on the train and called Uncle John to meet her at the station.

"Yes, yes, yes, okay, okay. Ya, ya, okay," was all Uncle John could manage to say. Uncle John's head must have been jiggling like crazy.

"Thank you, sweetheart." Aunt Betty kissed Bobby. He made sure she got on the train.

One time I was in Times Square walking to Sam Goody's with a group of college friends when I spotted Aunt Betty, walking alone, swinging her pocketbook, and smiling at everyone. She had a pretend beauty spot on her chin and black stockings. Her hair was redder than I had ever seen it before. There was no mistaking what she looked like. *"Just walk right by, Jackie, don't stop,"* I said to myself. But she saw me. I was embarrassed by the way she looked, but my friends had the good sense to continue walking while I stopped to talk.

"How are you, honey, *Yet thet budney, halween hel wich.*" (My sweetheart, how pretty your face.)

As always, she was kind and loving. We must have made a funny pair there in the middle of Times Square. She hugged me and I hugged her. I felt uncomfortable and awkward, but even then, I felt love and compassion for Aunt Betty and I knew somewhere that she was not the happy person she presented to the world. We talked for a few minutes. I asked her about Carol and how she liked school. I excused myself and explained that I had friends waiting for me at Sam Goody's. Aunt Betty kissed me again and said something in Arabic that I think was a kind of blessing.

I felt some guilt about the embarrassment I had felt in front of my friends. I did love Aunt Betty and knew that she needed love from us.

Carol was a lot like her mother. She was energetic and full of fun. After we had all moved out of the Big House, we still met on Saturdays for the movies. We usually met in Uncle John's office. Carol would ask for money for the movies and Uncle John would give her a twenty dollar bill. In our family, we were given just exactly the money we needed, nothing more. Twenty five cents for the movie, five cents for candy and the bus fare to and from the movie.

Carol would buy us whatever we wanted. We would go to a music store and she would buy four of five of the same records and give one to each of us. We sometimes browsed in Kresge's Five-and-Ten. I loved bubble gum and blowing bubbles. Carol bought whatever I wanted.

Like Aunt Betty, Carol made up her own language. We didn't know what any of it meant, but we used it and laughed. It was whatever you wanted it to be. For example, *"Majapola and dadarie"* could mean "Hi," or "'Bye," or "This is great," or "This is stupid."

Aunt Betty and the children began to spend the summer months at the Beachwood Hotel in Old Orchard Beach, Maine. It was a favorite summer place for people from Montreal, and I think Aunt Betty felt comfortable there. They would leave right after school was out and stay until Labor Day. Uncle John visited them on weekends. Carol invited me to stay at least one week every summer and I went once or twice. Their family was so different from mine. Aunt Betty never asked where we were going or what we were going to do. And, she always gave us money to spend at the amusement center or for lunch on the boardwalk. My mother always asked where we were going and when we would be back, and money was rationed by an allowance. When the money was gone, that was it; we had to wait until the next allowance day. Aunt Betty had one hotel room for herself and Uncle John when he visited on weekends. The kids had a room to share. On one of my first weeks there, I opened the door to Aunt Betty's room by mistake. She was sitting on the edge of the bed crying. I shut the door quickly. I think she saw me, but she never said anything to me.

We had a great time doing everything we wanted to do. We played on the beach, we spent time on the rides, and we sometimes had to babysit Joey and Ginger, but even that was fun. Aunt Betty had her own routine. She never woke up early and never went to bed early. When the door was shut we knew not to disturb Aunt Betty. The door was shut almost every night, and the door was locked more than unlocked.

"My mother has lots of friends in the hotel and she likes to have them visit in her room," Carol said.

Uncle John would show up on Saturday morning, happy to see his family and ready to relax. The door was never shut when Uncle John was visiting. He and Aunt Betty would dress up for dinner and walk to the hotel dining room. He would stand up straight and put Aunt Betty's arm around his and prance down the hall. He almost giggled with delight.

He would leave Sunday night, content that his family was happy and enjoying the summer. Uncle John had the world he wanted; he created it. He colored it all wonderful, like frosting over a moldy cake.

At home in the A. John Ganem law office, life was not that smooth. Ganem's markets became the subject of an Internal Revenue inquiry in 1945. Uncle John was the keeper of all the business papers for the family. He took charge of the income tax filings for the business. He was also supposed to draw up wills for Sitho and everyone else in the family. He never did. He had a huge safe in his office and only he had the combination. In the safe, he kept deeds for different properties, tax returns for the businesses, and other documents that needed safekeeping.

"He fucked it up, just like he has fucked up everything he's touched," my father told my mother. "He's going to get us all thrown in jail, the stupid bastard."

"Can't you set up a meeting and see what's really going on?" my mother asked.

"Adma, he doesn't know what's going on, that's the problem. He's so Goddamned stupid. He doesn't even know what his wife is doing, let alone the business."

Agents of the Internal Revenue Service arrived to audit all of the books. They plunked themselves down in Uncle John's office and the office of the business and stayed for months reviewing them.

Uncle John's attempt to help was to ask Tommy Lane to step in, but what could he do? He had just been released from jail for income tax evasion.

"How stupid can he be? We should let him go to jail," my father said to Uncle Bill about Uncle John.

Uncle Bill had a stroke the year before and was struggling to understand the world around him. My father talked to him as if he was okay and he wasn't. The men in the family business met several times to talk and to try to understand their options in this family mess. They couldn't talk to each other. They were never able to calmly discuss anything. Two or three civilized sentences were about all they could manage, and then the shouting would begin. Uncle John had never had any verbal skills. He grunted, stuttered and made noises resembling words, but few people understood him. Because the businesses were thriving for a long time, no one thought to change legal counsel.

It served him well to be incoherent. He had made a mess of all the legal papers in the family. In the chaos, it was generally thought that he put a few pieces of property in his name alone.

The audit by the IRS marked the beginning of the unraveling of the family. Slowly, the glow of success began to dim. The joy of the Big House disappeared. And with the same speed of their success, there was a spiraling down that couldn't be stopped.

Chapter 16

Disillusionment

The Ganem family owned the Big House for seventy-five years. Today, there is one woman who lives in that very big house. She is the widow of my father's youngest brother, Emil, the doctor. How she came to be there is a long story, part of which explains the implosion of what was once a close and caring family.

Uncle Emil's education was paid for by his brothers. He went to Andover Academy, Harvard University, and Johns Hopkins Medical School. He was intelligent and ambitious. He was also arrogant and greedy. He interned in Hartford, Connecticut at the Hartford Hospital. One of his fellow interns was the brother of Katharine Hepburn. Uncle Emil went to the Hepburn's house for dinner many times and met them all, including Katharine. He told that story all the time.

In the years that we lived in the Big House, Uncle Emil was away at school except for holidays and, even then, he spent most of his time in his room studying. We never really knew him. We knew only that he was very smart and very special. He never had to work in the business, even during the summer when he was home. He was treated differently from everyone else, in every way. When it was time for him to marry, he did a scan of the area Lebanese women who had been to college. There weren't that many at that time. The best qualified was Arlene Corey, who had graduated from Radcliffe College. It didn't get much better than that.

Uncle Emil was snappy and sarcastic with all of his nieces and nephews. He made us all feel uncomfortable and asked questions just to make us feel stupid. He wanted to ensure his intellectual superiority in the family. When three of his nephews went to Andover he was visibly soured. And when cousin Kenneth went to Harvard and asked Uncle Emil for a letter of recommendation, he suggested that Ken go into the family business instead. Ken went to Harvard and to Harvard Medical School. Uncle Emil had very little to do with him after that.

We all thought that he was probably a very good doctor. He was a urologist and worked at the Massachusetts General Hospital in addition to his private practice in Lawrence. He could be totally charming and witty with his patients and fellow doctors. They didn't know the Emil we knew.

Aunt Arlene moved into the Big House after they married. Aunt Julia and Uncle Bill were still there, and Aunt Blanche, Aunt Margaret, and Sitho were there, too. Aunt Arlene was always whining,

"How can I entertain our doctor friends in this house with any privacy?"

"I'll need to change this old-world furniture before I invite anyone to visit."

Most of the business had moved closer to Boston, so Uncle Bill and Aunt Julia bought a house in Swampscott and moved out of the Big House. Aunt Blanche and Aunt Margaret went to work every day and that left Sitho at home with Aunt Arlene. Aunt Arlene didn't speak much Arabic, so Sitho spent much of the day in her room. Aunt Arlene never stopped complaining. It was her major topic of conversation, even with Sitho. She didn't like the furniture, the floors, the old kitchen, even the walk in refrigerator. It was shut down and a new regular refrigerator was bought for the pantry.

The Big House still stands. It's hollow and empty of the great energy and hope it once held. In some ways, the family's dreams came true. But the insecurities of the family toward the new world they had entered turned inward and created a place of deceit and mistrust.

I have since visited the Big House. I have driven up the long driveway and circled around the back to look at the small orchard, the big garages, the work shed, and the stump where Sitho used to kill the chickens and turkeys. It is all still there, but shabby and overgrown with vines and moss. There's no life there. I'm not sure what I feel when I look at the house. There is an ache and a sadness. The house held a dream, a very big dream. It was filled with great promise and expectation of a new and wonderful world.

On the big front porch, behind the columns, there are big moving boxes. The boxes have been there for years. The last time I was inside the house was about thirty years ago. My mother and I went to pay our respects to Aunt Arlene, my uncle's widow. She said she was going to remodel the whole house. The kitchen had been torn apart. The floor was stripped of the linoleum and only bare planks were left. She was also lowering the ceilings in the living room, so beams were installed and nothing more was done. We think she still lives there.

As the family had grown more successful, it had also grown apart. There were no more Sunday dinners and talent night shows. Three families moved out and left; the only ones left were Sitho, Aunt Blanche, Aunt Margie, and Uncle Emil and his wife, Aunt Arlene. Sitho began to feel uncomfortable. Her job of cooking and managing that big household was over. Aunt Arlene was not the same as her other daughters-in-law. She talked differently, too, in a half whisper.

One of my aunts said, "She went to Radcliffe, they all talk that way there."

Sitho stayed in her room more and more. Finally, Aunt Blanche, Aunt Margie, and Sitho moved to Marblehead. Sitho seemed out of place there. She belonged in the Big House; she was the Big House. She never seemed the same in Marblehead.

Seventy-five years ago, the neighbors didn't want a Lebanese family moving in. The Emersons and the Stimsons objected to the foreigners. The Ganems bought the house using a "straw man" to avoid confrontation. Equal housing laws did not exist at that time. Over time, the neighbors learned to like the big family in the Big House. They were invited to the Fourth of July festivities. They were invited to the Christmas tree lighting. And, of course, they enjoyed the abundant food that was part of every event.

In those early years, everyone pulled together. There was little time for anything other than work. Everyone worked all the time. The business grew and investments were made in property in and around the City of Lawrence. John was charged with all legal matters. It wasn't until many years later that the brothers found out that John took care of nothing but himself and his family. There was no estate planning. There were no proper books kept; there were no partnership agreements drawn. The Big House was initially in my grandparents' name, then in the sons' name; then in just Emil's name.

My father would do all the dealing to buy cars for the whole family. He would go to a car dealership and negotiate a good price for sometimes as many as five cars. The money came out of one big pot. No one asked questions about the one big pot. How much was in it, is it divided evenly among everyone? Does it go to the last one standing?

As the Big House emptied, the brothers grew apart. They grew wary of each other; they mistrusted each other. There were attempts made to sit down and talk. But communication never came easy to any of them. There were those among them that had a lot to hide, and the abrupt meetings served them well.

Sitho was never told about any of the problems of her family. As always, they protected her. Sitho was always in a very special place with everyone. I believe she knew that her family had changed. Even after she moved to Marblehead and we went to her house for special holidays, the feeling among the brothers was strained. Although Sitho didn't understand much about the business world, she knew down deep that everything was not okay. Gido had died in 1945, before the trouble began. I think the family would have protected him, too. My father believed that you can trust only your own family, but he lived to see that this was not so. It was the biggest hurt of all.

The house in Marblehead was of average size. It had three bedrooms, two bathrooms, a living room, a dining room, a den and a kitchen. Sitho never looked comfortable in that house. She was alone all day. She watched some television, but it was just to have voices in the house since she didn't understand English. Everyone visited Sitho, but it wasn't the same. For one thing, we couldn't all visit at once; we had to take turns. She was away from everything and everybody she knew. She couldn't even get to the Lebanese church in Lawrence anymore. Father David came to visit her once in a while and I'm sure she was comforted by that. Sitho died in 1954, less than two years after the move. Her wake and funeral were held in Lawrence at Saint Anthony's church, which was near the Big House she loved. Her friend, Father David, presided.

Just before Sitho's death, Uncle John the lawyer decided that it would be the right thing to do to sign the Big House over to Uncle Emil and his family. My father objected, but was out-voted by others in the family. Uncle John took care of things he had no right to meddle in and neglected those things that he was responsible for. Uncle John was supposed to have made a will for Sitho and he never did. He was supposed to have created wills for everyone in the family. My father pushed him to do the work after Sitho died, and John said he was going to get to it, but he never did. My father died in 1955 without a will and with unsettled estate issues still outstanding for Sitho.

Uncle John thrived in the chaos he created. My father used to call it hocus pocus. He babbled and threw out legal terms meant to confuse. He took very good care of himself and no one else. Just before my father died, he and my mother went to the Registry of Deeds to check on ownership of some of the Ganem properties. What they discovered was that most of the properties were in Uncle John's and Uncle Bill's names. My father went directly to Uncle John's office and demanded an explanation from him. Uncle John was always shaking his head and moving his eyes everywhere instead of focusing on the person with whom he was talking. He moved papers frantically around on his desk, opened the huge safe that was in his office, and moved papers around in there, too. My father shouted and got red in the face. John shouted and shook. There was no resolution, except that my father and mother decided that day that my father would have to get some help to straighten out the mess.

The toughest part of all for my father was the realization that even his oldest brother, Uncle Bill, had not been straight with him. There was no one in the family he could trust or turn to for help. He was heart-broken and enraged. He had worked hard his whole life and had been duped and used and taken for a ride. The only people he trusted had let him down.

He died in September of 1955, two months after discovering the deceit. My sister Mimi was home when my father died. My brother Bill was in the army serving in Germany, and my brother Allan was at Wharton School in Philadelphia. I was out for the day, looking for a job after college graduation.

Many times after my father died, my mother would say, "You were your father's favorite, Jackie. He never wanted to visit anyone but you when you were all away at school. He never missed a Father's Day event with you."

He loved the Father's Day weekends. He was more outgoing that any of his family. Meeting new people was fun for him. Men especially related to him, because of his sense of humor, a kind of teasing way that worked well to establish an easy relationship. One afternoon in the fall of my sophomore year, the dorm attendant called me to tell me that I had a visitor in the living room. I could not imagine who would be visiting me during the week. It was my father. He had never done anything like that before, especially without my mother. As I recall, he was going to New Jersey to pick my mother up from a visit with her sister. We sat for just a few minutes and talked; nothing important, nothing urgent, but it was very special for me. I treasure the memory.

My father's wake and funeral are still a blur to me. I didn't cry much then. It was only years later that the enormity of my father's death became real and I could grieve.

Chapter 17

Transitions

I have thought a lot about the impact of my father's death and the changes it brought to all of us. The hopes and dreams of my brothers were crushed. There would be no business for them to come back to and no guidance from my father. Mimi was only fifteen when he died. She was at Abbott Academy in Andover and unsettled about what college she would attend. I took her to visit colleges, and she chose Smith. Mom asked me to drive her there when school started. There were no trips to fancy dress shops as there had been for me. My mother was lost without my father. He was her support, her shoulder to lean on, and her protection. It was my father who gave her the strength to do all that she did.

The summer before my father died I was dating a lawyer from Springfield. He wanted to marry me. He gave me a diamond ring in July. I knew I didn't want to marry him, but I had some hesitation. In those days, women were supposed to marry right after college. It was the expectation. My father came home from work the next day having been told by my excited mother about the ring. He was a man of few words. He said, "Jackie, you don't have to marry him if you don't want to." I gave the ring back. He knew I had to hear that. Going forward, I would not have my father around to help me, to counsel me as only he could. We were on our own to manage as best we could.

Before my father died, I dreamed that there would be a place in the business for me. That dream gave me great confidence. The death of my father forever changed the trajectory of my life. I was lost, too, in so many ways. I felt derailed. It took many years to have that insight and to come back to the person I should have been. I was walking in shoes that were not mine. These uncomfortable shoes forced me to smother the dreams I had and be some other person.

There had always been such great security in our large, successful family. After my father died, everything changed. The fundamental security was still there, but without him we were on our own to deal with the family. My uncles called for a family meeting to talk to my mother about what life was going to be like without my father. I was the only one home, so I attended the meeting. They explained nothing, but simply declared to my mother that she would have to manage on far less money now that my father was gone. Furthermore, she would have to go to Uncle John's office to ask him for money, tuition, bills, expenses for the house, everything. I asked a question and was told "This is none of your business." That statement was from Uncle Emil, the doctor who was educated at Andover, Harvard, and Johns Hopkins by the generosity of my father and his brothers.

In the beginning when the world crashed on us, there was no clarity, only confusion. Then slowly there came a time when survival became paramount. We do what we must to get through and move forward.

Canterbury Street house

Aunt Malvina with me Aunt Mabel,
Mom with Billy and Aunt Emma with cousin Joyce

Me and Billy on the driveway of the Big House

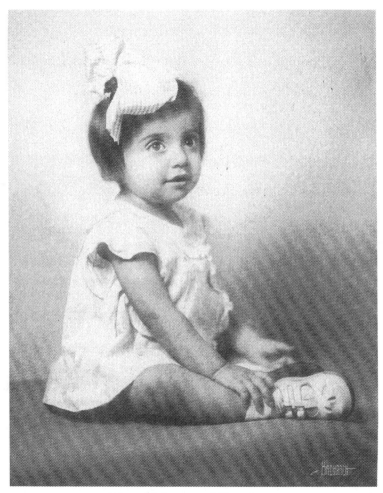

Me with bow and Dutch cut
1935

Dad in front of the Corey's Berkeley Street house
1934

The Big House

Dad, Gido, Uncle Bill, Sitho with Uncle Kamel, Uncle John 1906

July 1931
Mom, Dad, Aunt Emma, Uncle Bill, Aunt Julia, Aunt Emma,
Aunt Blanche, Aunt Betty, Uncle John

Mom
1935

Me, cousin Joyce, Billy, Allan and Mimi in front of the
Corey Berkeley Street house

Mrs. Cole's kindergarten

Kendall Hall

"Life must go on; I forget just why."

—Edna St. Vincent Millay

Chapter 18

My Mother and Me

After my father died, mother and I were alone together. We had our own private pain. We never shared much before he died. His death just thickened the wall between us and made sharing impossible. We lived together, but alone.

Friends and relatives called and visited to pay their respects to my mother. She was always contained. I knew she was suffering. I couldn't help her; the walls were too high for me to climb and I was afraid. I was afraid for her and I was afraid for me. My brother Billy was still in the service and my brother Allan and sister Mimi were away at school. I didn't have a job and I didn't know what I wanted to do. I did know that I didn't want to be home. The house was big for just the two of us, but not big enough. I never felt that I had any privacy. The house was full of grief and painful memories. There was no way to push them away. I felt like I was drowning.

Friends visited. We would go to the beach or the movies. But I always had to come home. Most nights I would come into the house with a date to sit and watch television or just talk.

"Does your Mother have company?" Bill asked.

"Yes, I think my Uncle is visiting," I said.

I could hear my mother talking to herself, going on and on about being cheated by my father's family. I knew there was no one else in the house. I would turn the volume up on the TV to drown out her voice. It didn't work for me; I still heard every word she said. I would go into the kitchen to see if I could stop her or at least quiet the voice. She would be sitting with a full ashtray of cigarette butts and a half empty bottle of

Seagrams, puffing and pointing across the table as she made her case to my father's brother, "John the Bastard," as she called him.

"Mom, it's late, let me help you up to bed."

"Those sons of bitches, Jackie, they won't give us your father's share of the business. What am I going to do, what are we going to do?"

Oh, God, who cares! Just stop this shit! Please! Please! I just wanted out of this whole scene, and fast.

"Mom, Bill's out on the porch, he thinks there is someone else here with you. Could you please not talk so loudly?"

"He would understand. Maybe he can help. Tell him to come into the kitchen and have a drink with me."

"No, Mom, please, you're in your nightgown and you've had too much to drink already."

She stood up after two tries and walked to the cellar door.

"I'll get my robe from the basement."

Before I could stop her she opened the door, took two steps, and fell down the flight of stairs. I ran down after her and saw that she was covered in blood from a cut on her head. Bill heard the fall and was there beside her. We wiped the blood and found the cut on her scalp.

"This is bad, Jackie, she'll need stitches on that cut." He was always so calm and cool. That drove me crazy, really. I gave him the name of our doctor, who lived just around the corner. Dr. Feldman lived in the same house with his office. Bill called and Dr. Feldman told him to bring my mother to the emergency room at Lynn hospital and he would meet us there.

I got my mother dressed in something other than her nightgown. She was quiet now, no more talking to "John the Bastard." I know she was embarrassed, but I was so angry and embarrassed, too, that I could feel little compassion for her. She was trying hard to be sober, but the few words she managed were slurred and unintelligible.

Bill was much nicer to her than I was. We brought her to the hospital and Dr. Feldman met us. He knew the story. He'd probably patched other people up in the middle of the night. My mother was filled with remorse and was totally docile. Dr. Feldman had to shave a big section of my mother's hair to do the stitching and, for more than a month, my mother wore a hat or scarf in and out of the house until some hair grew back to cover the scar.

She continued to have long conversations with my father's brothers in our kitchen. Months went by and Bill asked me to marry him. I felt the same way I had felt many times before in my growing-up years. There was no real reason to say yes; and really no real reason to say no. I felt vulnerable and without defense. I never made decisions. I just fell into them. I married Bill that same way.

I always knew I was married to the wrong man. And now, many years later, I know that I married him for the wrong reasons. The feeling was buried, but it simmered at the base of everything.

"He's a good man. He's got a good job," my mother said.

I couldn't think about anything. Until this time, there wasn't much thinking I had to do. Decisions were made for me. I went to Kendall Hall in Peterborough, New Hampshire because my cousins went there. The school counselor recommended that I go to Connecticut College and I did. I never even chose my own clothes, my mother did.

"Four unsettled children, that's what I've got. That's what your father left me with," she would say.

I never answered her. What could I say?

I felt numb and that is how I managed. It's not a pretty state. Numb protects but it also limits. I couldn't feel anything. When Bill came along and he was a "good man" and had a "good job," that was enough for me.

I lived on Tums for the next three months before we got married. My stomach was never settled. So this is what love is all about—getting the ring, planning the wedding, and deciding on the guest list, the food, and the flowers. Bill and my mother did it all. Even the ring was not my choice. My mother knew a dealer in the jewelers' building on Washington Street in Boston.

"We'll go there to get the ring," she said to Bill.

"We'll look at them, Adma, but I may not want to buy it there."

"Don't worry, Koppelman will give me a good deal. We've bought lots from him in the past. I'll take care of it."

Neither one of them asked me what I wanted to do. And anyway, it was my father who always did the deals, not my mother. I took more Tums and drank my tea. I couldn't drink coffee anymore, because it bothered my stomach too much.

We went to Koppelman's the next Saturday. My mother had called to make an appointment. He buzzed us in and we went up in the old fashioned elevator that barely held the three of us. There was the beginning of some tension between Bill and Mom.

"We're not going to buy the ring here if I don't like what I see. I just want you to know this before we get there," Bill said to me. I wish he had said it to Mom.

"Hi, Adma, how are you?" Koppelman said, "So sorry to hear about Louie. He was a helluva guy. Tough, but honest. Just what I like. So you've got a wedding coming up. Wonderful, wonderful. Lucky man." Looking at Bill he said, "Wonderful family, don't come any better." Bill and Koppelman shook hands, and then Bill introduced me.

"You look just like your father. Did he ever like talking about you. You must have been his favorite." I swallowed hard to keep from crying. I so wished my father was still here. I knew I wouldn't have been sitting there if he was still around.

We followed Koppelman into his private office and he shut the door. He had a nice face, gentle and soft. When he sat down at his desk, he looked like he was part of the furniture. He was my father's friend and I liked him immediately. There were two very large black safes on one of the walls and a cabinet with many small drawers on the other. There were big windows that looked out onto Washington Street. His large oak desk was bare, except for a large square of velvet with a jeweler's glass on it.

"Sit down, sit down. Now, what kind of diamond are you looking for?" He looked at me. My mother answered. I was glad she did. Bill answered, too.

"One at a time here," he said. "Let's start with Jackie. This is going to be your ring, after all." There was a pause. "Well, let me take some stones out first and see what you like, then we can look at some settings."

Koppelman went to one of the safes, opened it and pulled out a tray of loose diamonds. He went back to the desk and began to put them on the velvet cloth. He put the jeweler's glass in his eye and carefully examined them, describing each one as he singled them out.

"This is a two-carat blue diamond with only a small flaw off the right of the center. This is a yellow diamond of good to very good quality. You'll want at least two carats. That makes a beautiful ring, especially if you want a solitaire setting. It has to be two at least to look like anything. Take a look at these."

He handed them to me. I looked at them and then passed them to Bill. My mother got them last, but looked at them much more closely than either Bill or me.

"How much is a two-carat diamond?" Bill asked.

"Depends on the quality, but roughly you could say $1,000.00 per carat, then you have to figure in the setting and baguettes, if you want them.

"Wow," Bill said as he pushed back in his chair.

"Is that your best price?" my mother asked.

"Just a minute. Adma, can I talk to you outside the office for a minute?" Bill said. He was angry that my mother was taking over the deal. He stood up and left the office. My mother followed, making noises of apology to Koppelman.I wanted to say that I didn't give a shit about the ring, but once before I said that to my mother and she gave me a long lecture on why I should care. She said, "Of course you care. Why shouldn't you care? Don't tell Bill you don't care."

Bill and Mom came back in a few minutes, both a little red in the face.

"Now, what were you saying about the settings and the baguettes?" Bill asked.

I managed to engage in some of the decisions. One baguette on either side of the two carats in a platinum setting. The ring would be ready in three weeks.

Although everyone said it was a beautiful ring, I never felt comfortable with it. It just didn't feel like me.

Chapter 19

Company

We married February 4, 1959 and bought a new house in Topsfield, Massachusetts. I continued to work for New England Telephone until Andrew was born in November, 1960. Anne was born in February, 1962. I was busy and very happy being a mother. Clearly it was a full time job with little time for anything else. Bill was recruited and offered a bigger and better job in Hartford, Connecticut with Pratt and Whitney Aircraft. The offer was too good to pass up.

We moved from Topsfield to South Glastonbury Connecticut. Bill decided that renting for a year would be wise. He had been working in Connecticut for six months and was sick of the commute on weekends, and I was tired of nonstop baby talk and the commute. Andrew had just turned two and Anne was walking at ten-and-a-half months. On weekends in Topsfield we either made love or argued. There was no middle ground. By Monday morning we were both glad to separate for the week.

It was late November when we finally made the move. I knew no one at all. The neighborhood we moved into was very rural. There were as many dogs and horses as there were people. I could see my neighbors' houses in November, because the trees were bare. But in the spring when the trees were in full bloom, we were alone in the woods.

Because we were renters, the neighbors had little or no interest in meeting us and making us feel welcome. It was an older group, anyway. Their children were all in school and some were older and off on their own. I liked the house. It was small and manageable—three bedrooms upstairs with a full bath, and downstairs there was a living room, dining room, small kitchen, and a half bath. The backyard had a clearing before the woods took over and the clearing was fenced in, which was perfect for Andrew's playpen on nice days. I could watch him from the house and, for an hour most days, he was happy and safe.

We had moments of excitement. Andrew locked himself and Anne in the upstairs bathroom, and then turned the water on in the tub and the sink. I could hear the water running and called to him to unlock the door. There was no sound except for the running water. I had wild images of what was happening and, after pounding on the door for a few more minutes I could wait no longer and broke the door open. There they were, happy, happy babies playing in the water. Andrew had squeezed toothpaste all over the mirror. Anne had pulled herself up and splashed in the toilet water. The tub water was still running, but they were safe. The only damage was a broken lock on the door.

Then there was the day that we walked into the back yard near our neighbor's corral, and Anne climbed under the fence and found herself standing under the belly of one of the horses. The neighbor came to the rescue. I apologized and thanked him. He was not too happy with us, and he never bothered to introduce himself.

But the most fun of all was when Bill's brother Bob and his family came to visit. Bob traveled for the State Department in a function we never understood. He married Liliana from Equador the year before and had a baby about Anne's age. Bill invited them to spend Christmas with us, that is, not just Christmas but ten days. We didn't know anyone in Connecticut and we didn't really want to cart Christmas with the kids to my family in Massachusetts, so having company for the holidays seemed just fine. It was fine for about a day, but then it wasn't fine at all.

The evening of the first day was like having company for dinner. I cooked baked stuffed shrimp, which Bill said Bob really liked and, of course, we had gin martinis. Andrew and Anne liked the company, who seemed more interesting than mom all day and just dad at night. Their little baby, Bobby, was cranky so he didn't go to bed early; he stayed with his mother and father all evening and went to bed when they did at about midnight. Bob seemed to be the primary parent. Liliana drank martinis and talked about Equador and how much easier life is there than in the states. She had maids, cooks, and drivers and lots and lots of jewelry. She showed me the jewelry she had with her, which was just a dot compared to what she had at home in Equador. I was polite and said "ooh" and "ahh" when I should. I wasn't really interested, and never have been very interested in jewelry of any kind. She didn't understand that at all, and I don't think she believed me.

I cleaned up the dining room and kitchen. Bob gave Liliana the baby to hold and he brought a few dishes to the sink. The evening was over and it was fine. Bill was pleased with the dinner and the evening. He loved his brother and wanted to show him a good time while he was visiting. We gave Bob and Liliana our bedroom and put a small portable crib in the bedroom for little Bobby. I was not happy giving up our room and told Bill. He said, "I never see my brother," and "It's only for a few days," along with several other reasons that made me feel sufficiently selfish, so I agreed.

Bill and I slept in Anne's bedroom. It had twin beds, which were more like cots with thin mattresses and metal wires underneath that poked through the mattresses. We didn't really sleep, we just napped during the night. Anne had never been a good sleeper, and our presence in her room was just enough to keep her up and babbling. It was fun for her.

Lucky Bill got to go to work every day. He called at least twice a day to see how things were going. Bob and Liliana slept late with little Bobby. That was the good news. When they did get up, life got very busy. For one thing, baby Bobby was not happy with us. Bob and Liliana used a pacifier dipped in honey to make him happier. And that was fine with all of us except that honey was dropped all over the house. Everywhere I went either my feet stuck to the floor or my hands stuck to every surface I touched. The honey was all over our bedroom furniture. Anne was intrigued with the pacifier, and every chance she got she pulled it out of Bobby's mouth. It had a nice little ring on it, perfect for her little hands to hook onto and pull. She'd pull and he'd scream. Then we'd have a scuffle, I would rescue the pacifier, Liliana would yell something in Spanish, and Bob would yell something back and pick Bobby up to quiet him. I apologized the first dozen times or so, but then just took the pacifier away from Anne and popped it back in Bobby's mouth. Sometimes that worked, but mostly it didn't and he gagged on the pacifier, spit it out, and cried.

I asked Bob and Liliana to make themselves at home and help themselves to anything they wanted in the refrigerator. The first day or two I offered to make them breakfast, but Bob said he would take care of it. Actually, he took care of most everything anyway, since Liliana didn't cook or take care of the baby. He managed in the kitchen with just an assist from me about where everything was located. Somehow, after they had eaten, they got too busy with other things to clean up. The "other things" were Bob's bathing Bobby and Liliana bathing and getting dressed. They spent afternoons Christmas shopping or sightseeing. At least they were out of the house.

Dinner was mine to do. At first it wasn't too bad. I would put Andrew and Anne to bed. Then I would have a martini and pretend civility in the living room with Bill, Bob, Bobby, and Liliana.

Bill would shoo Bob and Liliana away after dinner saying, "Oh, don't worry about cleaning up. Jackie and I will take care of it."

Well, it was mostly Jackie who took care of it, and I got good and sick and tired of doing the whole thing myself.

Bill had a friend in Glastonbury that he had known from a previous job in Massachusetts. His name was Werner and his wife's name was Evelyn. I had met them once and they seemed like nice people. They were nice enough to invite all of us to dinner, without the babies. I wanted to shout, "Yippee!" What a break it was for me to have dinner made and no clean up to do. I worked hard at getting a babysitter; I even interviewed a couple of them. The wife of the real estate agent we rented the house from agreed to the job. He undoubtedly assumed that there might be another commission down the road when we bought a house. She would drive over at six o'clock on the appointed night and I would review the house and baby needs with her.

I was tired, but glad to be getting out. We were all set, except for Liliana, who was still getting ready well after six o'clock and well after the babysitter briefing was done. Deciding what jewelry to wear was a major project requiring a long conference with Bob, then with Bill, and finally with me. I put on earrings and a watch, and I was ready.

"You look great," Bill said.

"You look beautiful, Liliana," Bob said.

I said nothing, but I did think to myself: *And what about me? What do I look like? Don't I look great too?*

"Come on let's go. Jackie, get that bottle of wine we are bringing to Werner's." Bill held the garage door open for Liliana and Bob while I went back for the wine. As I walked back, the door was shut in my face.

"Hurry up Jackie," I heard from the other side of the door.

I opened the door and went into the garage thinking I would get in next to Bill, but Liliana is sitting in my seat.

"Get in the back seat, Jackie. Hurry up, we're late."

"I will not get in the back seat."

"What do you mean? Get in the back seat now."

"I will not get in the back seat."

"What's wrong with you? Get in this minute."

"I am not getting in the back seat. Maybe you should go without me."

"Liliana is cold and she's not used to the cold. The front seat is warmer for her."

"Oh, of course, I see. Did you hear *me*? I said I'm not getting in the back seat."

I could see his rage. I could feel his rage. But he could not see mine. There was a carriage beside the car. Bill picked it up and threw it against the back of the garage.

"That's it. Go without me. And, oh, here's the wine." I tossed it across the hood of the car and he caught it. I turned and went into the house.

Over my shoulder I said, "Don't follow me. I am not going, period."

I went back into the house and slammed the door. The babysitter was surprised to see me, although I'm certain she heard the whole garage scene. I apologized to her and paid her what she would have earned if she had stayed the whole evening. I heard the car back out of the garage and watched the headlights go down the driveway. Bill was driving faster than he usually does, and there was some snow and ice on the driveway, so he was skidding from side to side. Liliana may have been warm in the front seat, but she was certainly frightened there, too.

I have no idea what Bill said to Werner and Evelyn. I didn't care. We didn't talk about the evening. I didn't ask and they didn't volunteer. Bill was angry with me, but I was angry with him, too. I had never been as bold before; it was a new me. He didn't like the new me at all. I liked the new me, but it was too new to really be me. The feelings were different and didn't quite fit, but deep down I took some pleasure in the change. It would take a very long time for the different pieces to make a whole.

Two days later Bob, Liliana, and Bobby left us. I had to drive them to a hotel in Hartford where they would take a limo to the airport. Bill was not talking to me very much and, for some reason, decided that I should drive them to the hotel. I think it was my punishment for being a bad girl. Of course I had to take Andrew and Anne with me. I got lost going to the hotel and coming back. Many years later I learned that Bob and Liliana and Bobby were late getting to the airport, missed their flight, and stayed at a hotel at the airport. They never called to tell us.

Chapter 20

Life With Bill

Bill walked in the door from work at the same time every day. He did the same things every day when he came home. He would find lint or crumbs on the floor and pick them up as he came in. God, how that pissed me off. He didn't say anything. He just picked up what he found on the floor and threw it away.

He might just as well have said, "What the hell have you been doing all day anyway?"

I tried to talk to him and tell him how it made me feel to have him do that every day. He listened, I think, but never said anything. I let it go for the most part. I loved my life with the kids and it was full with the pleasures of seeing them grow, change, and be who they were.

Bill had a way about him that filled the house when he was in it. He never seemed to be part of the flow of the family, but was more like the supervisor. There was Bill and then there was me and the children. We were his job and his responsibility, but we were also a chore and a burden. I felt it and the kids did, too. It was not a nice feeling. And everything was important to Bill. Everything had the same level of priority. When everything is important, nothing is important. We had no gray in our lives; only black and white.

The Catholic Church was important to Bill. Rules and regulations of any kind were important. We all went to church on Sunday. What a job that was. The kids never wanted to go and neither did I. Bill got himself ready and then waited for the rest of us.

Anne: "What shall I wear? I hate this dress. I'm not going to wear it."
Andrew: "I don't want to go."
Anne: "I'm not going."
Andrew: "I have a stomach ache. I think I'm going to throw up."
Bill: "Jackie, hurry up. We'll be late."

Despite pushes, shoves, and braiding hair in the car, we made it to the church. After Sarah was born in 1966, she and I would sit in the baby room behind glass so we could see and be seen. It was sound proof so the cries of babies and mothers didn't disturb the holiness of the others. Of course, the mass was piped in so we wouldn't miss anything.

Some time in the early '70s, the church proposed a drive to unite families by aiding them with their communication skills. It was a new initiative from Rome. The father of every Catholic family went to a tutorial on the topic. Then, over a period of several weeks, the father was to hold a series of meetings, asking questions of each family member to open communication.

"Sunday afternoons from 1:00 p.m. to 3:00 p.m. we'll sit in the living room and talk. This will be good for all of us," Bill said.

"I don't want to talk," Anne said.

"You have to talk," Bill said.

"Dad, I want to be outside with Kenny. We're finishing the tree house with Mr. Karwoski," Andrew pleaded.

"You have plenty of time during the week for that business. This is important for all of us and we are going to do it."

"Bill, can't we do it some other time—maybe after dinner for a half-hour or so during the week," I said.

He looked at me and said nothing.

We tried it. It felt like we were sitting with a gun to our heads having Bill say, "Talk! You will talk. What are you thinking? What are you feeling?"

"So Anne, what's on your mind?"

"I don't want to be here. That's what's on my mind."

"That's enough of that talk. I'll have none of that!"

"You asked me what was on my mind and I'm telling you. I don't want to talk and I don't want to be here. That's what's on my mind."

"You go up to your room until you can behave yourself."

"This is stupid," she said. "Andrew, isn't this stupid?"

Andrew didn't move. Bill stood up and went over to Anne.

Anne ran upstairs. "I still think it's stupid, and you're stupid too."
She slammed the door to her room.

We stayed in the living room and tried to talk for another few minutes. That was the first of only two sessions. The second one was no more successful.

"Bill, we can't force these things. We should be talking to the kids all the time. We should be listening to them all the time, not just for a little while on Sunday afternoons. It's too fake."

"That's part of the problem here. You aren't behind this thing and they know it. And Anne, I'll break her if it's the last thing I do."

"Bill, do you hear yourself? You're going to break her? She's eight years old, for God's sake."

"That's what I mean about you. Did you hear her say this is stupid? And I suppose you think that's all right. Well, it isn't all right."

"You know, Bill, if you could just relax and enjoy the kids instead of always trying to teach them something. They are wonderful children. Why can't you see that? I know Anne is tricky, but she's always been her own person."

"That's the trouble with you. You're too easy on them. 'Her own person?' What does that mean? What kind of people are they going to be without discipline?"

"I give up. How can I talk to you about anything?"

I couldn't listen anymore and I couldn't talk anymore. We'd had this conversation more times than I could remember. It went nowhere. Most of the time I didn't get an answer at all.

It was right about this time that I began to write letters to Bill. I thought that if he had a letter he could read, re-read, and think about, it might help us begin communicating. I wrote long letters. They were pleading and pathetic.

Bill,

I keep trying to reach you, but you can't hear me or you won't hear me. You forget that I'm on your side. I am your wife, your partner, working with you to make a good life and to raise our children together.

They are wonderful children, but you don't see that. Is it that you are afraid if you show some gentleness, some love, some enjoyment that something bad will happen? I feel that somehow we get in your way. You make me feel like we are all a burden to you. Dinner should be a time to share the day with everyone and instead, it is a series of orders or directions to all of us about what we should say, how we should say it, or what we should do at the table. There is no joy here.

Please, please take time to enjoy life, enjoy your family. I try very hard to make life good for all of us. I wish you could see that. I wish you could see me, and see Andrew, Anne, and Sarah. I love my family; I want you to love us, too. You have made a good life for us and it breaks my heart that you cannot take pleasure in any of it.

I want to hear how you feel. I want to hear what you have to say about what I have shared with you here. Please talk to me.

Jackie

Bill,

I am desperate. I have written several letters. You have taken them to work with you and I assume you have read them, but you haven't said one word to me. I called you at work today and asked you what you thought about my letters, and all you could say was that they were "interesting."

I am incensed by the word "interesting." It is about us, about our family, our lives, our lack of connection with each other, and all you can say is it's "interesting." Don't you feel anything? Don't you care about me, and how I feel? Don't I count for anything? Do you care about how the kids feel about you, about us? I wanted to hang up on you when I heard "interesting." We're not talking about a movie or a book; we're talking about us, who we are, how we are. I'm telling you I am not happy, that I feel like a non-person with you, and all you can say is "interesting?" I am in a rage and it's just "interesting" to you.

(No signature)

Bill,

You said the marriage was everything you ever wanted. You said you were happy with your life. You told me you love the children and our life.

You told me you loved me. But that is all about yo;, what about me? You see no reason to change anything, because everything is exactly what you want. You're still not listening.

Bill, I think we should make an appointment with a marriage counselor. We need help. I want to fix our marriage and maybe a counselor will help.

Jackie

"You've really gone off the deep end, a marriage counselor! I told you there is nothing wrong with our marriage, didn't I? I'm not going to talk to anyone about anything."

"Bill, this is just what I've been telling you. You think there is nothing wrong and you have everything you want in our marriage. But I don't have what I want. Please, let's go see someone. We can't go on like this."

"Oh, God, you are so dramatic. 'We can't go on like this.' Why? You have it so tough, is that it? You have three children and a beautiful house. What else do you want? I'm not going to talk to anyone and that's final. Everything is fine."

Everything wasn't fine, but we kept going. Divorce was not in my mind then. I sometimes wondered if other marriages were like ours and that maybe that's just how they all were. I spent a lot of time listening to the conversations of our friends. How did they talk to each other? Did I hear any intimacy between the husbands and wives? Could I hear love and what did that sound like? I think intellectually I knew that ours was not a good marriage, but I was too busy to think about doing anything about it.

I kept writing letters; Bill continued to find them "interesting." Sometimes he would say, "I'll think about it," but that's as far as it ever went.

"That's it, that's all you can say? Do you think I'm right about our relationship? What am I supposed to think if you don't talk about it? Don't you care about it?"

"Of course I care about it. What do you want me to say? You know I love you and the kids. Do I have to talk about it all the time?"

"That's not it, Bill, it's so much more than that. Is that what you think I was writing about? Let us in, talk to us."

"For God's sake, Jackie, let it go!"

My teeth would clench. I wanted to break something. Shake him, hit him, wake him up. Slowly, I would just let it go. Is this how it's supposed to be? I was too busy to spend too much time on any of it, and I let myself back into the routine until something else triggered the rage. It was a rage of frustration at not being able to penetrate the walls around him. It was a rage that he ignored me and dismissed me. I didn't count.

The marriage was okay until it wasn't okay anymore, and that happened after Sarah got sick. I have wondered sometimes if we ever would have divorced if it weren't for Sarah's illness. I don't know the answer to that. I do know that when we divorced, Andrew, Anne, and even Sarah were not surprised. They have told me this. They were waiting for the end of the marriage.

We went to counseling near the end of the marriage. Bill was all for it, but it was too late. By then, it was not marriage counseling, but divorce counseling. We made some awkward and perfunctory gestures at trying to communicate. The counselor suggested that we try going on dates as a way to reconnect with each other. We tried that more than a few times, but I was finished trying. There were too many unanswered letters, too many one-sided attempts, and too much pretending to myself and everyone else. Sarah's illness woke us all up and there was no going back.

Chapter 21

Sarah

Sarah tried to kill herself in October of 1979. She was thirteen years old. It is only now that any of us can look back at that time and see it. We can see now how we were all changed by the event. We can't understand it, we can only know what happened to all of us because of it.

It is only now, too, that I realize how sick Sarah was and what a miracle it is that she is fine today. Dr. Boynton, Sarah's psychiatrist, said to me many times in those five years how strong Sarah was.

"She's not as fragile as you think she is," she would say.

How little we know about each other. I didn't know Sarah at all. I knew her only as my youngest child, who was working hard to be all things to us. She got all A's in school. She played basketball like her sister Anne and the trumpet like her brother Andrew. She tried to always do the right thing. She never wanted to cause any trouble. She worked hard to be the perfect child, and she was.

What did we miss? We should have seen signs of problems. Were we too busy to notice? Did she have nightmares we ignored? We never saw unhappiness in her. She worked very hard at hiding her demons. Suicide attempts are not flashes that appear suddenly; they are years in the making. We saw none of it.

Mostly, this is my story as Sarah's mother. But it is also our family's story. Change came to all of our lives because of Sarah.

Life was chugging along in Glastonbury—not too happy, not too sad, but it wasn't just right, either. Andrew was away at Gettysburg College in Pennsylvania; Anne was finishing high school; and Sarah was thirteen and in the eighth grade.

Bill and I had fallen into a low-energy relationship. There was really no interest between us, except in the three children we shared, what they were doing, how they were doing, and what we should be doing for them. I had always needed more than the relationship was giving me. I ran a nursery school for five years. I tried very hard to get a teaching job, but there were none around at the time. I finally got a job with the local telephone company, Southern New England Telephone (SNET).

The first job I had there was entry level, from 9:00 a.m. to 5:00 p.m., so it was okay with Bill. His life was not impacted at all. I still did all of the things I always did to keep life going without change.

Sarah was an excellent student. She was sweet and caring. Friends called her "Sarah pure heart" or "Sweet Sarah." She was a wonder to me—so unlike her father or me and so unlike her brother or sister. At first I was concerned about working and not being home for Sarah when she got home from school. Anne was busy with sports and her art work until close to 6:00 p.m. every day. Sarah would be home at 2:30 p.m. and was alone until 5:30 p.m. She constantly reassured us that she was fine. She never wanted us to worry about her.

I did worry about her. I had a low-level anxiety. It was nothing I could identify, at least not at first. I called Sarah every afternoon to see if she was home and okay. She had stopped being best friends with Julie next door. I wondered at this, but let it go as teenage angst. Although Sarah always stayed up late at night, the hour got later and later.

Sometimes I would wake up at 2:00 a.m. or 3:00 a.m. and her light would be on. I would go into her bedroom and tell her to go to sleep. She would say she was reading a good book and wanted to finish it. This was not unusual, but it was happening more frequently.

In late October, we went to Parent's Weekend at Gettysburg College and Sarah came with us. She absolutely adored her brother Andrew. She loved everything about him. He was gregarious and friendly and had a wonderful sense of humor. He was a star trumpet player all through high school and college. She laughed at all of his jokes and loved all of his friends. She had a wonderful time all weekend. Andrew's friends treated her like their very own little sister and she loved it. The weekend was a happy one, and we all felt good Sunday night when we returned home.

I was feeling a sense of calm when I went to work on Monday, although from about 4:00 p.m. on, most of my recollections are foggy and still carry great sadness as if I see them through a wall of tears.

"Jackie, your daughter Anne is on the phone. She's crying and wants to talk to you right away." The voice came from the desk next to me. I jumped up and took the phone.

"Mom, Sarah cut herself. Her throat is bleeding!"

Oh, God. Get home . . . no . . . Call Bill . . . Call 911 . . . Call Dr. Walker. No, this is going to be okay. No it isn't! Just get home. How could this be? How could this happen? Sarah . . . Oh god, Sarah. It's a mistake, an accident. Of course, this isn't really happening.

But, it *was* happening. I called Bill. Bill called Jim Walker, our pediatrician. I drove home in a blur of fear. Bill was there before me. The bleeding had stopped but bloody towels seemed to be everywhere. I took Sarah in my arms.

"I'm okay, Mom, I'm okay," she said. There was a blankness about her. Anne was shivering. Bill held her.

Dr. Walker had told Bill to bring Sarah to his office and he would meet us there.

"I'll talk to Sarah alone. Why don't you two go and get something to eat or a cup of coffee."

We couldn't leave. We waited in his empty office. He talked to her for what seemed like hours, but was more like a half hour. He came out alone and told us that Sarah had to go to the hospital that very night and that he would stay with her in the office while we went home to get her some clothes. She could not go home. She could not be left alone. Sarah had cut her throat with a razor. She had also cut her wrists. He told us that she was hearing voices that told her to kill herself.

What does this mean? Will she be okay? Why does she have to go to the hospital tonight? How long will she be there? Will she be okay? Can I stay with her? Will she be okay? Oh, please, will she be okay?

There were no answers.

Sarah went to Hartford Hospital that night. I stayed with her. And I stayed with her the next night, and the next night until other plans were made. She didn't talk very much, and, when she did, she tried to comfort me.

"I'm okay. Don't worry, Mom."

She stayed in bed. She slept most of the time. The nurses would come in and check on her. They were giving her a sedative of some kind. Jim made arrangements for Sarah to be admitted into the Mt. Sinai Adolescent Psychiatric Unit. This was a short-term facility mostly used for evaluation.

The day she was admitted we were told that she could not have visitors, but that we could talk to her on the phone if she wanted to talk to us. She didn't.

I remember as sharply today the very moment Jim spoke with me about Sarah and her hospitalization.

"She's very sick, Jackie, and may need long-term hospitalization beyond Mt. Sinai. She's hearing voices and she's trying to kill herself. We need to protect her. She'll need one-on-one supervision."

I know Jim said much more to me then, but I couldn't hear anything after that. I remember that I was standing and felt weak and had to lean against the wall and then Jim. I was blind with tears.

I know they are wrong. They can't be right. Oh, God, what is this? Someone else, somewhere else . . . Empty inside. Can't hear anything, can't see anything. What is long-term? Is it six months? Is it a year?

I felt like a part of my life had been taken away from me. A piece of my heart was gone. I ached inside all the time. There was no way I could understand.

At the end of three months, we met with the hospital staff and with Jim Walker to talk about Sarah. I heard only pieces of the conversation. My anxiety blocked my hearing. I can't tell you where that meeting was or who was there. I heard only sharp words coming at me, like knives, each one cutting me.

"Sarah can't go home. She's a very sick young lady . . . needs long term care . . . structure . . . twenty-four hours per day, seven days per week . . . Yale Psychiatric Institute . . . Institute of Living . . . the Menninger Clinic . . ."

Words, words, words.

We didn't consider the Menninger Clinic. We couldn't have Sarah that far away from us. We had two other options, both highly regarded. One was Yale Psychiatric Hospital in New Haven and the other was The Institute of Living in Hartford.

My head was full and empty at the same time. It was full of fear and guilt and questions. There was no clarity. It felt empty because I could not see or hear anything. I moved through the days doing the same ordinary things I had always done, but without thinking or feeling anything. Sarah's illness was so big nothing else mattered.

We visited both hospitals with Sarah. Doctors at each place talked to Sarah alone. I knew Sarah was very sick. As days went by and we saw her more, we could see changes in her. She was sinking deeper and deeper into a dark depression. Her long red hair that we all loved was now worn over her face. She was hiding from us and from the world.

Yale Psychiatric Institute was just a building—one building with sterile walls and cold, barren rooms. What were we supposed to see? What were we looking for? How were we supposed to know if this was a good hospital for Sarah? We met and talked to a doctor. Sarah had her own separate interview. Yes, he thought this would be the right place for her. He talked about adolescent problems.

"I have seen some people here that don't look like adolescents; they look much older than Sarah," I said.

"We don't think about chronological age here. We have some patients who are thirty and older, but they still have adolescent problems," the doctor answered. I had no idea how to evaluate him or what he said. I didn't like him. Bill was better than I was with asking questions. What could I ask? "Can you help Sarah?" "Can you make her healthy again?" There was no answer to that from anyone.

We took Sarah to the Institute of Living in Hartford. It was a complex of ivy-covered buildings behind a brick wall with manicured lawns and shrubs. There were trees and benches and even a swimming pool. It looked like a college campus. It was a peaceful place to those looking from the outside.

The interviews were no different from those at Yale, but the Institute was only twenty minutes from home and that made us feel better and closer to Sarah. Strange how big decisions are made.

In the four-and-a-half years Sarah was there, the pool stayed empty.

Dr. Boynton was Sarah's psychiatrist. We met her and other aides on the Monday night in January that we brought her there. It was dark and cold outside and dark and cold inside. That night at the Institute, Sarah sat in a large leather chair looking away from everyone. Her hair fell over her face.

Dr. Boynton told us that Sarah was going to be in the most secure unit in the hospital with one-on-one supervision twenty-four hours per day, seven days per week. I remember saying to the doctor that I was sure Sarah didn't need that kind watching. Dr. Boynton simply said, "Yes, she does." My fear and anxiety was so great that to this day I have a freeze-frame picture of two very large, faceless men, one on each side of Sarah taking her away from us.

This was the beginning of a long journey for all of us. Sarah went to high school at the Institute. It was a small school: one small building where all four classes of high school were taught. The program for Sarah was paid for and supervised by the town of Glastonbury.

There was nothing ordinary about what we did or how we felt. I had little energy for anything else. I moved through the days and weeks struggling to balance job and family, carrying a profound sadness that never left me.

Although Bill and I shared the heartache of Sarah, we grew apart. For me, it was a private pain and private awakenings that over time created an infinite distance between us that we could never bridge.

The Institute of Living high school on the property wasn't really a high school; it was a building that housed the school for all of the young patients at the Institute. There were only a few students in any of Sarah's classes. It was more like having a private tutor.

Sarah went to the Institute school for four years and graduated. Over the years, we were invited a few times to see the accomplishments of the students. The faces of the other students are a blur. I only saw Sarah. I was never relaxed when I was at the Institute. My stomach felt tight. I could only look straight in front of me, neither left nor right. I felt fear every time I was on that campus. I think Bill was better than I was. He managed to talk to some of the others at the school. I never could.

We missed all of Sarah's growing up years. Anne and Andrew, too, no longer knew Sarah. Even now, they struggle in some ways to know her. She left our house a little girl, the baby in the family, and after she left the Institute she went to college. She never came home. She never had the chance to establish herself in the family mix. She works hard now at doing that. It feels like Andrew and Anne have kept her in their minds as the baby sister. They love each other, but at times it is not an easy relationship.

I never had any long conversations with Sarah's doctor, but I know now that Sarah was never scheduled to come home to live with us again. She could not do that. It would not have been the best thing for her. I see that now. Sarah needed distance from all of us. Somehow she could not be Sarah when she was with us. It was tough for all of us to be individuals. Toughest for Sarah, who strived always to be perfect.

Dinner was never fun for any of us. Bill used dinner and our being together to teach us lessons. Good manners, for instance, were a topic every night.

"Don't speak with your mouth full."

"Take your elbows off the table."

"Please, thank you, excuse me, may I please" on and on.

If there was an attempt at conversation it never went very far because Bill always found a reason to interrupt.

"Take your hand away from your mouth. How can we hear you with your hand there?"

"Stop tapping your foot on the chair. Sit up and sit still."

Anne was the only one who worked hard at changing the ritual at the dinner table.

Bill:	"Jackie, get me a glass of water."
Anne:	"Dad, you didn't say 'please' and anyway, why should Mom get you a glass of water? Why don't you get it yourself?"
Bill:	"That's enough of that from you young lady."
Anne:	"You tell us to say 'please' all the time and you never say it. It's not right. It's not fair!"
Sarah:	"But . . ."
Andrew:	(quietly aside) "Shhhh. Sarah, don't say anything now. Dad's going to get mad at you, too."
Bill:	"Not fair, not fair—I'll teach you to speak to me that way. Get up to your room right this minute and stay there. Jackie, get her up to her room right now. No dessert."
Anne:	"Why should I? I didn't want dessert anyway."
Bill:	"One more word and you will stay in the house every day after school for a week. I mean it."
Anne:	"One more word."
Bill:	"That's it, that's it. Up now. Jackie, get her up in her room right now. Move."
Sarah:	"But Dad . . ."
Andrew:	"Sarah, shhhh."23w
	Anne would leave the table with a burst of energy, pushing her chair hard against the table.
Bill:	"I'll break her if it's the last thing I do. You make sure she stays in this house every day this week after school."

"Bill, please . . ."

"Don't 'Bill please' me. You heard me. She's got to learn who's boss here and she's got to learn not to talk back, period."

Sarah: "Dad, do you want me to get you a glass of water?"

Dinner was this way most nights in our house. Andrew always tried to keep peace. It didn't work. Sarah wanted to do the right thing always. It was hard to know what the right thing to do was in our house. Bill shut me up the same way he did the children.

Chapter 22

Altered States

We watched Sarah change. Slowly we realized how very sick she was. We didn't know her. She was too far away in her head for us to see her. She tried so hard each time we saw her to make us feel better.

"Don't worry about me, Mom. I'm okay. I'm going to be okay."

I know I must have had a look of despair on my face. I felt a tension so intense each time we went to the Institute that I could not look around me, only down or straight ahead.

The first few months at the Institute of Living were the longest and hardest. Sarah was on watch for twenty-four hours, seven days per week. Someone was with her all the time. Even so, Sarah managed to hurt herself. She was in the most secure unit of the hospital. To get to the unit, it was necessary to pass through two locked doors before reaching her. The common room was always filled with smoke. There were only twelve patients in the unit but every one of them smoked all the time. Sarah smoked one cigarette after another. She could not have matches; an aide had to light the cigarettes for her and the others. It must have been easier to just light them one cigarette at a time.

The common room had two couches and a few chairs lining the walls. There was a table with magazines and a rug in the middle of the room. At one end of the room there was a glass enclosure where the aides stayed. From there they could watch what was going on and take care of their paper work. There were four aides there all the time. They were young and I learned early on that they never had anything to say about Sarah, so I stopped asking any questions.

Sarah sat on the floor leaning against the wall of the glass aides' room. It was her favorite place. She would sit there smoking, her long red hair hanging over her face, looking down at nothing. She was the youngest patient in the unit. One of the patients danced all day to imaginary music. Others sat, not moving for hours at a time, smoking and looking at nothing. Sarah was on the drug Thorazine, which among other things caused the blank and distant look.

One day after Sarah had been at the Institute for a few weeks, she was sitting on the floor in her usual place leaning against the wall, hiding from everyone behind her hair. She was smoking one cigarette after another, putting the cigarettes out on her arms, up one arm and then the other. The smell of burning flesh filled the room and the aides' station. Sarah felt nothing. The aides smelled the burning flesh and found Sarah. They picked her up and brought her to a special room. She was screaming now, not from the burns but from some terrible hell in her head.

She spent the next two days in that terrible hell. She was put in a straight jacket twice. The strength she had was gargantuan, not that of a fourteen year old. Sheets drenched in cold water were used to quiet her and smother her demons. She was so physically hot that the sheets sizzled when she was wrapped in them. Steam rose from her body.

Dr. Boynton was called. We did not know the details of this incident for some time. We did know that Sarah had burned herself; we saw those burns. If we had any doubts about how sick Sarah was, those burns told us that Sarah was where she needed to be.

We didn't understand what was happening to Sarah, but I never let myself think that Sarah wouldn't get well.

Chapter 23

Change

Nothing stays the same, but Sarah's illness felt like a bolt of lightning to me and my life as it had been in Glastonbury. Everything had poignancy—a depth that made it impossible for us to feel light about anything. I understood then and now what having a heavy heart means. The passage of time lost its meaning. Days went by one at a time as always, with nothing but sadness to mark them. They all felt the same.

It was hard to care about anything. My energy for the stuff of daily life was hard to come by. Eventually, I had to face telling friends and family about what was happening to Sarah and to us. I called my mother first. She was visiting my sister. I went into a vacant office at work and closed the door. My throat was tight, and I knew tears were right behind. My sister answered the phone. She started with her usual questions.

"How is everyone? How's Andrew? Does he like Gettysburg? Is Anne the captain of the basketball team? And Sweet Sarah? The boys want her to spend a week with us at Christmas."

"Mimi," I interrupted, "Sarah is in the hospital." I can't really remember what other words I managed to cry out. My sister put my mother on an extension so she could hear what I had to say.

"She will be okay, won't she?" asked my mother with fear and uncertainty in her voice.

My sister couldn't think of anything to say but, "What about school?"

"Oh Mimi, I am talking about Sarah's life. I don't care about her missing school," I snapped. This was not like me, but I didn't care. The pain inside blocked me from feeling almost anything else.

In some ways, this defining time heightened and accelerated everything. The experience crystallized each relationship and gave each one new definition that may never have evolved without it.

I called my brother Bill that very same day. How remarkably different the call was.

"Oh, Jacks, I am so sorry. How can I help? Do you need money? Whatever you want, just let me know. You know I am here for you. Please, please let me help."

I cried, "Thank you."

"I love you, Jack."

I know I didn't really feel the love then. I couldn't. I think my mother told my brother Allan about Sarah. He didn't call me. I guess he didn't know what to say.

I thought we had a lot of friends in Glastonbury. We had only a few. Slowly, neighbors and friends learned of Sarah's mental illness. Some friends avoided us. Some wrote caring notes to me. I think it was easier than calling and talking. What do you say? How do you show you care or understand? I knew that contacting a friend in crisis was not easy. We all knew that. Reaching out is never easy. It frightens us. It leaves us open to hurt. There is also the mystery and fog of mental illness that makes everyone nervous. The "six degrees of separation" falls like a shroud on our instinct to reach out and comfort.

When years later I could look back with some clarity, I recognized those who cared enough to take the risk and still be a friend. It seemed like those people we counted as best friends were those that stayed away. I thought these were the people we knew best, the ones we could always count on to be there for us. We didn't know them at all. We had spent vacations together for weeks at a time and shared Saturday night dinners, parties, birthdays, and anniversaries. We shared most of life's happy times together. The memories now smack of an emptiness. My head and heart were too full then to feel anything about the loss of friends.

While Sarah was fighting for her life, we were fighting with our own demons. What did we do to Sarah? What kind of family are we? It felt like everything was up for grabs. There were no rules to follow. Nothing was sure or certain. There were only questions without answers.

We were not allowed to visit Sarah for three months when she first entered the Institute. I have a vivid memory of that visit. We parked the car in the parking lot across the street from the main entrance. There were never very many cars there. We went into the main foyer, the same main foyer we had been in three months earlier to drop her off.

I could not look around at the room ever. I focused only on the visitor desk and the woman behind it. It never, in four years, became easy to do. We asked for a pass to visit Sarah. The woman behind the desk looked up her name and wrote the pass. She then gave us directions. The unit Sarah was in at first was the most secure at the hospital, which meant that we had to go through several locked doors to reach her.

Neither Bill nor I spoke a word to each other as we walked across the grounds to reach the first building. There were a few people walking around. I could see them in my peripheral vision. I always thought that everyone I saw there was a patient. I never spent much time thinking about it. It took every bit of energy just to focus on the visit. I missed Sarah. I ached to see her. I was afraid to see her. I wanted to hug her and comfort her and love her. We didn't know what to expect. We were both quiet and privately fearful.

We were there, at the final unit door, and the aide admitted us after seeing the pass. I know the unit had windows in it, but it felt cellar-like inside. As always, the unit was filled with cigarette smoke. There was a glassed-in office where aides could watch the patients in a living room area in front of them. I looked only between nervous blinks at the patients in the room. There was no energy there. Maybe there were four of five young women in the room. They were staring blankly at the floor or their hands or feet. One woman was wildly dancing around the room. No one looked at her and she never stopped moving the whole time we were there. They were all young, but not as young as Sarah. Sarah had just turned fourteen.

Sarah was in her room just off the larger room we entered. An aide was with her. Sarah had an aide with her twenty-four hours a day, seven days a week. It must have taken every ounce of energy Sarah had to see us. I know now that she tried hard the few minutes we were there to make us feel okay about how she was.

I didn't cry but I must have looked like I was going to. "Don't feel bad," Sarah said, "I'm okay."

When Sarah said that, I knew she was not okay and knew, too, that she needed to be right where she was.

We didn't talk much. Bill held Sarah's hand for a long time. The pain in the room was suffocating. I took Sarah's other hand in mine. I kissed it and held it to my cheek. As I did that, I saw some red sores on her wrist. I later found out from Dr. Boynton that Sarah had started to smoke and had put the cigarettes out on herself. This was one reason she was put on one-on-one supervision.

Sarah was on large doses of Thorazine. This was the drug most commonly used at the time for people who had lost touch with the world. It was a powerful drug that put Sarah in a removed place, out of touch with us.

This first visit may have been thirty minutes or three hours. Time lost all meaning when we were there. We kissed Sarah goodbye. I didn't want to leave her, but I didn't want to stay there either. I felt uncomfortable when I was there, except for the times that we were with Sarah and could touch and hold her. We walked back across the grounds and into the main building again to drop off our pass at the reception desk. Neither one of us spoke. We were lost in our own pain, our own questions, and our own longing for Sarah.

We all fell into a routine without Sarah at home. We knew she was being cared for at the Institute. There was a hollow place, an emptiness in our hearts and our house without her. We didn't talk about it much. We talked about the easy things such as taking care of the paperwork with the insurance companies, and buying Sarah clothes and other things she needed. The tuition for Sarah's schooling at the Institute was paid for by the town of Glastonbury. We had to go to a meeting with the teachers, counselors, and others from the Institute to discuss the need for Sarah to qualify for the town's support. The people at the meeting were kind and generous. Sarah's teachers knew Sarah only as a very good student who never caused problems. They knew Sarah as we did. The psychologist from the Institute spoke. I don't remember what he said. There were sounds of disbelief in the room. Then the meeting was over and we left the room. Bill and I walked through the halls of the school. We didn't look around and we didn't speak.

We thought we knew Sarah, but we were forced to step back from her and look again. We weren't supposed to be separate now. We knew she needed to be away from us, but that didn't make it any easier for us to understand. We lived one day at a time.

As time went by and Sarah was moved to a more open unit at the hospital, she was allowed to come home for visits. We didn't know what to expect. We wanted the visit to be good. We wanted her to feel comfortable, but we wanted it to be special, too. *What should we have for lunch? What will she want to do? What does she like or not like?* I realized that I didn't know that much about her anymore. I knew she had become a vegetarian and I knew she smoked. I was feeling insecure about everything. The only thing I knew was that I loved her and I wanted her to be home again.

Sarah looked different, too. She had pierced ears—not just one, but maybe ten holes in each ear. Sometimes she wore one earring, sometimes ten. She also wore lots of makeup: dark eye shadows, rouge—sometimes brown, sometimes red—and lots of lipstick. Her clothes were different. The Sarah we knew only wore simple things like plain sweaters or shirts. It would be hard to describe what Sarah wore. She always seemed to have many things on all at once—pants with a long skirt, a blouse with a vest and a sweater, and a jacket. It looked very complicated. I could tell that Sarah loved the way she looked. It was not a look you would ever see in Glastonbury.

Chapter 24

Church

I never had a close relationship with the church. Growing up we went to church once in a while. The church we attended was Saint Anthony's in the Lebanese section of

Lawrence on Elm Street. Father David was the Pastor. He was a friend of the family.

He spoke English just a little. The mass we attended was in either Latin or Arabic, so we understood none of it.

Father David came to our house every Sunday for dinner. He knew we didn't go to church every Sunday, but he didn't seem to care. My father and his brothers gave money to the church, and my Uncle Bill was the head of the lay group that helped manage the church. It was an easy relationship. We never felt guilty about not going to church.

My father greeted Father David every Sunday with, "How was business today, Father?"

And then there would be some jovial talk between them about the collection basket and ways to improve the giving. If Father David ever said anything about my father's lack of attendance, my father's standard response was, "Beware the man in the front pew."

Sitho went to church every Sunday. One of her sons would drop her off, or sometimes one of my Aunts would go with her. On major holidays, like Christmas and Easter we always went to church. It would have been disrespectful toward Sitho if her children and grandchildren didn't go. Still, it was a casual thing.

All of the people that belonged to Saint Anthony's church were Lebanese. It seemed to have more to do with being Lebanese than being Catholic. The social events of the church seemed more important than the religious events. People helped each other. If my father had jobs available in his business, the first place he went for help was the church. If someone needed a doctor, there was sure to be one in the church. Most needs of the community could be filled by someone in the church or at least a connection to someone who could help. The church was there to help everyone in everyday ways.

The church that Bill knew was not like Saint Anthony's. There was nothing casual about the church for Bill. It was serious business and it was very important. Just like most of my married life, I did what I was supposed to do. I didn't think about it, I just did it. I sometimes think I checked my brain at the altar when I got married. That suited Bill just fine.

There were some exceptions to the "I just did it" rule. One of those exceptions was birth control. We tried to talk about the whole issue, but Bill was unyielding in his view.

"It is against the rules of the church to use birth control. We would have to go to confession and confess to the priest."

"Bill, look around, do you think that our Catholic friends with one or two children don't practice birth control? Of course they do."

"You are such a smartass about this stuff."

"No, I just know that if we don't want anymore children, then that is what we have to do."

The talk went on and on and always ended with Bill saying, "I'm not going to talk about this anymore."

I went into the "don't ask, don't tell" mode. I took the pill and never asked or told. I know Bill knew that I was on the pill, but he never said anything about it. I guess he thought that if he didn't talk about it then he wouldn't have to confess the sin to the church. After all, he wasn't taking the pill, I was.

Many years went by. I was still taking the pill, but I hadn't been to confession for as many years as I had been taking the pill. Every once in a while Bill would suggest that we all go to confession. I managed to find a reason why I couldn't go. For one thing, I really had nothing to say in the confessional.

"I used the Lord's name in vain?"

"I disobeyed my husband?"

"I coveted by neighbors husband?"

I must have been feeling magnanimous in 1979, because I said I would go with everyone to confession. I also must have had some kind of brain lapse, because when I got into the confessional, the only thing I could think to confess was the birth control sin.

"Bless me father for I have sinned. I use birth control."

There was a pause behind the screen. I thought I heard a sigh.

"How many times a week?"

"How many times a week?" I repeated.

"Yes, I need to know how many times." I think I heard another sigh.

I don't know what I said. I do know what I thought. *The priest wants to know how many times? Is that how many times we had sex? Oh, Jackie what a stupid woman to have confessed it in the first place.*

I bolted out of the confessional. I must have looked stunned. I felt stunned. I didn't bother to go up to the altar to say my penance. I really thought that if anyone should have to say penance it should be the priest behind the screen.

Later that day, Bill asked what had happened, and I told him.

"Don't ask me to go to confession again. I did my last one today."

We dropped the whole topic of birth control and confession.

When Sarah was first at the Institute of Living, we were looking for answers.

We looked at everything in her life. We looked at everything in our own lives. Sarah was going to confirmation classes at St. Paul's church in September 1979, in preparation for her confirmation in the spring of 1980. She had talked often about the priest that taught the class. She liked him. Bill thought we should make an appointment with him, and that maybe he could tell us something, anything about Sarah that would help us understand.

Bill called the rectory and made an appointment with Father Foley for a Wednesday afternoon. Father Foley was very young, a new priest and also new to the Parrish. I arranged the afternoon off from work. Bill came home, picked me up, and we drove to St. Paul's church in the center of town.

We didn't talk in the car. In those early days of her illness, I was always a minute away from tears. It was easier not to talk. Sadness surrounded us. The pain was numbing.

We parked the car in the rear parking lot and walked around to the front of the church. The rectory was next door. Bill rang the doorbell and a woman answered.

"We have an appointment with Father Foley," Bill said.

"Come right in to his office. I'll tell him you're here."

The office smelled like incense. It was dark with dark things all around—dark books in the bookcase, dark curtains on the windows, and Holy pictures and crucifixes all around. It was intimidating sitting there as we waited. I have no idea how long we waited. It could have been five minutes or an hour. It was so still and we were so numb we could have been suspended there for a very long time and not have known it.

Father Foley walked in and said, "Mr. and Mrs. Weatherwax, how nice to meet you."

He put his hand out and shook Bill's hand. He smiled at me, then went behind his desk and sat down. He looked younger than I had imagined, maybe mid to late twenties. He had a fresh, clean look that made him look younger and better looking than he really was. His hair was freshly combed.

"You wanted to talk about Sarah? She's such a smart young lady."

"Well yes, father, we want to talk to you about Sarah. She's not well and we thought maybe you could help us," Bill explained.

"Whatever I can do, I am happy to help."

"Sarah's at the Institute of Living in Hartford. She's sick, father, very sick. She tried to kill herself and now . . ." Bill couldn't say anymore. There was silence, and then Bill went on.

"She liked her confirmation classes with you. She talked about them every week when she came home. We thought maybe there was some light you might shed or something you observed. She liked you very much."

Father Foley adjusted himself in his chair, put his shoulders back and leaned forward toward us.

"She liked me? What did she say about me? What did she like in particular?"

Bill looked at me for the answers. I was speechless.

"Father, we wanted to know about Sarah in the class. How was she with you and the other kids? Did she participate? Did she seem happy? What did you see?" Bill continued.

"Well, I thought that if you could tell me what Sarah liked about me and liked about the class it would help me with my teaching and being able to reach these young people. Did she like the text? It's a new one this year. Did she like my style of teaching? It's important to be able to relate to them. I think I do that quite well, you know, I'm young and maybe that's what she liked. I've heard that before from some of the other kids."

He leaned back in the chair and seemed to forget we were there. His eyes looked up at the ceiling as he smiled and tapped his fingers together.

I was in a rage inside. I looked at Bill. Bill was going to try again, but I stood up.

"I think we should go," I said to Bill.

Father Foley was still in his reverie and still looking up at the ceiling, smiling and tapping his fingers.

I stood up, and then Bill stood up. At last, Father Foley released his gaze at the ceiling and looked at us.

"Maybe I could visit Sarah at the Institute. She might like that."

"No, no, I don't think so. Thank you." I said.

"She can't have any visitors, at least not yet." Bill said.

I don't remember saying anything else. I walked very quickly out of his office, through the hall, and out the front door. Bill stayed back and probably shook his hand again and maybe thanked him for his time.

I walked around the church and to the parking lot behind it and waited by the car for Bill to come and unlock it.

"Dammit, does he have to lock the car all the time," I said it out loud.

I watched Bill walk toward the car. He looked pale. His head was down. He unlocked the car door and we both got in.

I stopped going to church.

Sarah in her own words

Three months into my visit, my stay, my extended leave of absence, my rest, my recuperation, my five year fucking holiday into the land of the have-nots and the horrible, the mentally-maimed, the reality-challenged, I sat in a corner smoking a cigarette. I sat in a corner on the floor, me and my lit cigarette. I sat on the floor in a corner, at the end of one hallway, at the beginning of another hallway, around an L shaped bend by the fishbowl office.

I was quite near the office, but out of sight. On the wall above me was a mirror, the one used for plucking facial hairs and eyebrows and applying make-up when Cabinets were open. It was not allowed to take your make-up into the bathroom, or your tweezers into the bedroom, no no. I remember buying Q-tips at Here It Is my first week. I asked for one at Cabinets and was told those had been taken from my shopping bag by the staff. You see, once purchased, items were put into bags labeled with our names and given to staff to inspect and control as needed. Q-tips were not allowed on this unit, ever. Not even in Cabinets. It takes only a second to jam one into your ears, causing permanent damage to the eardrums and even if staff are near, there is only so much they can do to keep someone from harm. There is only so much anyone can ever do.

I was mad. I wanted my Q-tips. I should have been told what I could and could not have before I spent my parents' money. Or, seeing as each restricted unit shopped separately, not mixing with the higher-up patients, the Here It Is Ladies could tape a list on the counter near the cash register. Thompson I Restricted Items: Q-tips. Then they could tell us, "You're not allowed to buy that." My Q-tips were taken and never returned. I thought in jails you got your stuff back at the end, your pennies and pocket lint. I guess we didn't measure up to criminals. Hospitals, jails, all these societal caves, should have orientations for new people, or something typed out to read, like work places and colleges do.

But on this day three months into my stay at the new hospital, I sat in a corner alone, smoking. I sat in a corner alone, smoking. Nothing particular going on in my brain.

Not a wash of messy feelings, no, it was a day. A bland day in the middle of nowhere, containing a timelessness hard to decipher but really irritating at skin level. A nothingness, a bland empty opened in me and I sat enveloped in it, simply wondering about I and about reality. I understood that many older, highly educated people believed I did not live in reality. So I wondered where I was living. The thought reader, thought maker that I used to hear echoing off the insides of my skull was not prattling on. That robot-like, slow motion, monotone male pretty much stopped with his lists and commands as long as part of me seeped out onto the ground around me on a regular basis. And I think therapy and meds were fucking up his place in the scheme of things. I guess maybe *that's the point.*

Sometimes where that dull, empty, slow-like-mud thought dictator would have been, 'And now I lift my right hand and forearm. Now I tilt my hand to the right, to the left, to the right and to the left to physically indicate a greeting. Now I let my right hand and arm rest on my lap. She is approaching me. I will lift the facial muscles to either side of my mouth in an upward arc to physically mimic gladness. Now she is talking. I will tilt my head slightly to the right to indicate active listening. And now I—" and so on into eternity with his rhythmless, inflectionless chants, sometimes where the comfort of lists and following orders would have been, should have been in this continuing cycle, there would be a nothing. A whole, entire NOTHING. So much a nothing, the word is too much for it. Nothing was there. To write, "Nothing was there," means Nothing existed. And if even Nothing did not exist? Somewhere in there is the gap, the void, the huge blankness into which I fell, or into which I willingly stepped. Sometimes falling and walking are hard to distinguish for me, even to this day. Back then, I was teased for tripping all the time, tripping over nothing.

And so I sat and stared, trying to conjure up something, trying to pull a magic trick on myself. A trick, a trip into the here and now and TA-DA, I would exist, whole and unmolested from demons within or without. And I slipped into a soupy slop of soulessness, a split in the spirit, a split in the psyche and the less than nothing that held me here wanted a physical, a tangible way to get back. My magic back-fired and brought me closer to who I was. Not to a fictional whole self that, at most, existed in the future, but to my split self with thoughts and feelings miles apart, with spirit and body split, spilt in two and screaming a dry, silent scream, not motivated by pain, but by a want of pain. A want of something more than nothing.

I decided to chain smoke. I lit a cigarette with the end of the other and put out the old one on the inside of my left forearm. I felt nothing.

Less than nothing. Certainly not pain. I smiled to myself and rushed through cigarette number two to get to the good part again. To try again for something more than nothing. Cigarette number three, I didn't even bother to smoke.

I think it was the smell that alerted them. There was that, the smell, at least, if I couldn't have pain. Very unique, the smell of burning flesh and hair. And who would be so foolish as to do that sort of thing almost right next to the door to the office? But this was not planned by me. Nothing was planned. Planning by nothing.

This led to my first experience with wet-sheets. At CAPS, they used the traditional straight jackets. I am proud to say that when a straight jacket was used on me at the ripe old age of twelve, when I tried to rip open my neck vein with my fingernails, I burst out of the damned thing, ripped it apart and the staff had to put another straight jacket on top of the first one. I had my eyes closed when they pulled my arms, my weirdly long arms, through another set of Neanderthal-length, canvas sleeves. That was hot, two layers of army issue canvas. When I understood what I had done, when Lenny told me the next day, I was proud.

But here in the big leagues, it's wet sheets.

The patient is stripped completely naked and wrapped and rolled and wrapped and rolled by a number of very capable hands into tight, cold, wet bed sheets. I was a big, screaming on the inside, eyes closed burrito. My body was so hot when they did this to me, steam drifted up and away from my skin.

What is this? What is this thing of little ones hurting themselves, eating their way out of their own flesh?

When I was a wee one, real small, I had this dream. We all have those certain dreams or nightmares from childhood that we remember until death do us part from our bodies. One of mine, a recurring one, was me, me alone in a room, me alone in a chair, me alone in a chair in the middle of a room, me alone in a chair in the middle of an empty, windowless, not-quite-white room. There is a door, locked, locked with a bolt or with my mind, I don't know. I sit in a plain, wooden, straight-backed, no-arms chair. Nothing in the room, but me in the center, in the chair, the chair in the center of me and no way out, not even a window to look out and up at the sky from my point of view trapped in the center of the room. I stare straight ahead for a moment. Then I begin. I begin with my fingers on one of my hands, probably my

*right hand, my most capable hand. Then onto my hand, my forearm.
I am eating myself. Eating myself away into nothing. Getting smaller,
disappearing inwards, bye-bye. I have to eat myself, I can not bite off
and spit out. There must not be a mess, a mess on the floor, on the walls.
There must be no evidence I was here. I must be gone, get gone. No
screams, no cries, no pain. Persistent determination, focus, methodical
focus on the task to whittle away at me. There must be no mess. Who
would clean it up?*

*That was when I was small, little, seven, eight, nine, I don't know,
little, not too much to gnaw away, bones and all, crunch, crunch,
swallow, bite blood.*

*I remember, a waking memory, from when I was little, oh so small.
I was in the back seat of the family Buick, a deep green station wagon
with fake wood paneling on the outside. I was sitting in the back seat.
I got a window seat miraculously, for once, me, the youngest, didn't get
the middle. Maybe I had called it. "I get the window seat, I hozy, no
tops!" Big sister Anne in the middle, big brother Andrew on the other
side, Mom and Dad in the front. For those were their names back then,
Mom and Dad. We speed along in our rec-room for the road, over a
bridge, over a bridge we go. I think an image, I imagine, I feel it. In
my feeling image, I open the back door and tumble my wee body out
the door, into the traffic, maybe over the side of the bridge and down
and WEEEEEE!!! WEEEEEEEE goes my wee girl body, and WEEE
goes me into the no more.*

*I remember, a waking memory, the first time I brought one of these
images to life, into the land so many call the real world. I was small,
little, seven, eight, nine, I don't know. I'm in my room. I had my own
room in snotty, classist, conservative, uptight, snotty, fuck-you, get-real,
let-black-people-live-here suburban Connecticut. Dad was an engineer,
a top notch creator of jet engines, you see, with a math, design, make
things go brain like no one and could keep us all whole in our big yellow
house with the big green lawn. Mom had a nice lady job teaching nursery
school. And Dad had no clue about loving. He preferred to drink and yell
and make us all feel bad. I remember, a waking memory, being in my
room, when I was small, little. I had a wire hair brush for my long, thick,
wavy, auburn hair. "Redhead, redhead!!" every day at school. "Redhead,
redhead," turning my given beauty into bruises. I don't remember what I
was thinking, it was a plain day, a day, just a plain, hollow day. Maybe*

Mr. Monotone was there, I don't know, I can't remember which came first. But instead of brushing my hair, I looked at myself in my wooden wall mirror, same one Mommy had in her girl bedroom. And instead of brushing my hair, I tried my wire brush on the soft, white inside of my forearm as I looked at myself in my wooden wall mirror. A little blood, not much, just a touch, a few light scrapings, curly and thin like cheese from a grater, of my flesh on the brush, but I had begun. I had begun to try to claw my way out of me. And each time would increase in intensity.

And so, four or six of the staff wrap cold, wet sheets around my limbs. They all work at once. They are obviously trained professionals. One staff for each leg, one for each arm. One sheet for each limb. My limbs were wrapped and rolled and then sheets were wrapped and rolled around my whole body, pinning my legs together and my arms to my sides so I can't move at all. Two or three staff on each side. One side of my steaming body is tipped up, they pass the sheet under and pull it tight. I am tipped the other way, the sheet is passed over, pulled tight, tipped the other way, sheet passed under, pulled tight, tipped the other way, sheet over, pulled tight, tipped, under, pull, tipped, over, pull, tipped, under, pull, tipped, over, pull, tip, pull, tip, pull, tight, tight. A cocoon? Do I look like a cocoon except for the steaming head at the top?

Not quite alive, not quite dead, but an in between species. A mummy? Dead on the inside, nicely preserved on the outside. I felt like a plank of wood when they tipped and pulled, tipped and pulled. No ability to move. An inanimate object. An object. To be subdued. To be steamed. Steamed like a Chinese dumpling. An object. To be wrapped and steamed and then strapped to the steely, steel framed bed with four mammoth, airplane-sized seat belts. The seatbelt straps are permanently fixed to this steel bed, one at ankle level, one around the knees, one around the hips, one around the upper chest. I wondered where these specialty beds were made. Is there a Wet Sheet Steel Bed factory somewhere? Do they use recycled parts?

Voices poked through.

"She's so hot. I've never seen this kind of steam. Perhaps we should make them colder? Cool her down more?"

"No, she'll be fine. Sweat some of that anger right out. And if we make the sheets colder, her body heat might actually rise to compensate.

Her body is rebelling to protect her. It's okay. It's okay, Sarah. We'll watch you."

So I broke out of a straight jacket. And now I'm setting records with steam.

I was incredibly hot. I was hot and dry in the cold, wet sheets.

Six hours. At eight hours there is some kind of law, or rule. They must let you out, even if only to move your limbs. Some have been let out at eight hours, picked up where they left off with the violence and been wrapped right up again for another eight.

Six hours. Alone. Immobile. Hot. Thirsty. My memory of this is only aural. As when I was in a straight jacket, my eyes were closed the whole time.

I remember, about three, four hours in, dryly remarking inside my mind at the skill with which those hands wrapped me. They must have a lot of training to work here. Do they practice on dummies? Like people do with CPR? Is there a Straight Jacket Suzy? A Wet Sheets Wilma?

Chapter 25

Sarah's Book

Sarah eventually wrote her own account of her experiences with mental illness. I started to read Sarah's book for the first time several years ago when she visited from Toronto. I put it away. I didn't want to read it again, because it hurt too much.

Each time I read it even now, I ache for that little girl. How could I not have seen her pain, her downward spiral, her desire to disappear? Were we all too self-involved? We always said Sarah was the perfect child. How did she hide behind that image?

I remember that almost every day Sarah would wake up with a dream to share with all of us. It was her thing and we laughed at her retelling, the details, the drama, the intensity. I half listened between making breakfast and fixing lunches. Anne and Andrew laughed and brushed her aside as the silly little baby sister. Bill didn't listen at all.

Did she tell us about her dream of the little girl in the middle of the windowless room, sitting on a stool eating herself so she would disappear?

"Eating myself away into nothing," is what she later wrote in her book.

Did she tell us about her fantasy of opening the door of the Buick while we were driving, falling out, and ". . . there goes me into the no more"? Yes, she probably did. Did I hear them? Only a little. And if I did, I probably said some stupid, motherly thing like,

"Oh Sarah, you just had a nightmare. It was probably something you ate before you went to bed."

Sarah wrote that she could feel nothing. Is that what looked like perfect to us? She never complained, and she never argued with her brother or sister. She always did what she was supposed to do. But then she cut herself with her wire hair brush and put cigarettes out on her arm. She felt nothing.

"And Dad had no clue about loving," she wrote.

I felt this about him, but didn't allow myself to really think it. How did Sarah know? She was so young, seemingly so perfect, and yet she knew more than I did. She knew he had " . . no clue about loving."

Sarah felt nothing. "A whole entire NOTHING. So much a nothing, the word is too much for it. Nothing was there . . . Not quite alive, not quite dead, but an in-between species. A mummy? Dead on the inside, nicely preserved on the outside."

Me too, I was dead on the inside, but I didn't realize it until much later.

Chapter 26

Dealing with Reality

My job at Southern New England Telephone (SNET) was very structured. I sat at a desk all day and took complaints and orders from customers who wanted telephone service. I was never very good at it. I was all right with talking on the telephone, but I never mastered the details of writing orders. I called myself the "Queen of Blue Slips." Those were the correction slips that came back with almost every order I wrote.

I had been in the job only six months when our world crumbled with Sarah's illness. It was a twist of fate that the health insurance I had from SNET covered long-term mental health hospitalization. Bill's insurance covered only ninety days per calendar year. In quiet moments, when I allowed myself some comfort, I would look around at the sea of desks and think that I must be the highest paid person in the room. SNET was paying the Institute over $80,000.00 a year for Sarah's care.

The job gave some order to my life. I knew every day where I was going and what I had to do. I needed that. It was like crawling into a secure space where I didn't have to think too much about anything. I kept my head down and did the job. Then something happened that changed the calm.

It was sometime in May, four months after Sarah had been admitted to the Institute of Living. I was sitting at my desk doing one of the many mindless tasks that went with the job, when a fellow service rep sitting next to me tapped me on the shoulder to tell me that I had an urgent phone call. We were not allowed personal calls, but the word "urgent" felt like an electric shock through my body. I got up and took the phone from her.

"Hello, this is Jackie Weatherwax."

"Jackie, this is Dr. Boynton."

"Is Sarah all right? What's the matter?" I interrupted her.

"We don't know, she's run away from the Institute."

"What do you mean, she's run away. Where is she? How could she run away? Where would she go?"

"We are trying to locate her now. She left with two other patients here that were in the same unit with her."

"But the unit is always locked. How could they do that? Someone is with her all the time. Oh my God, is she all right? She's only fourteen years old. When did this happen?"

"They left last night when the aides on the unit were changing shifts."

"Last night? She was out all night?"

There was commotion around me. I could sense it, but I was blind to everything except what I was hearing on the phone. I remember that I was standing, but had to sit down as I listened to Dr. Boynton. My supervisor, Terry Croswell, approached and was flailing her arms.

"Personal calls are not allowed!"

I kept talking to Dr. Boynton. I waved my arm at Terry, pushing the air in front of her. Her face turned red. She was coming closer; she was going to put her hand on the phone to disconnect it. I moved around her to block her.

"Dr. Boynton, I will have to call you back."

I hung up the phone. I was in a rage. I was shaking. At that moment, I could have picked the desk up and thrown it across the room. I felt panicked by what I had heard. I feared for Sarah and her safety. I felt rage at Terry Croswell and rage at the world for everything.

I walked away from the main floor and into a small training room where I could call Dr. Boynton back. Terry followed me.

"Where do you think you're going? I will report you to the manager. We know you were on a personal call; the "observer" was listening in!"

"Do what you have to do. If you were listening in, then you know that the call was urgent and serious. I'll talk to the manager myself. Don't bother doing it."

I continued walking into the training room and shut the door behind me.

There wasn't much more that Dr. Boynton could tell me about what had happened. I called Bill to tell him. We cried together on the phone. Sarah and the two other patients were found the next day in Hartford. One of the other patients had friends living in an apartment in the city and that's where they stayed. Much later, we learned that Sarah had tried drugs and sex that night. She was safe and back at the hospital. That's all that mattered to us.

I began to change that day. The rage I felt allowed me to crack open. Although I had such great fear for Sarah and her safety, somehow I lost my own personal fear. It was like waking up from a long sleep or coming out from under a huge rock. I had an energy that was big and new. It was mine and it was not going to leave me.

Chapter 27

Cracking Open

While we were all focused on changes in Sarah's life, major changes were happening in my life. They were subtle at first. I was reconnecting with old friends that I had left behind when I married Bill. We were in a support group with parents of troubled children; I had begun personal therapy; and Bill and I were in family therapy, sometimes with Andrew and Anne and sometimes alone. I turned inward more and became self–focused. Work became very important to me. I wanted to prove to myself and the world around me that I was a successful person. There was a lot of anger in me, too. I was angry with myself, angry at what I had done, and angry at what I had not done. Rage is very energizing. I was going to show somebody, anybody what I could do.

I was promoted into a sales job in New Haven with the telephone company. It required three months of training. This meant driving an hour to New Haven everyday. At first I thought, *I can't do this. What if Sarah needs me?*

I spoke to Sarah's doctor, Dr. Boynton, and she said, "Jackie, you should take this job. This will be good for Sarah. She will see that if you can do what you want for yourself, then she will be able to do that, too. It is okay to have a life of your own. The message will be a good one for her."

How simple and yet, how profound.

At the time, Bill thought it would be good for me to keep on working. In May, 1981 I began a twelve-week training program for the new sales position in New Haven. I was given a company car to commute from home in Glastonbury to New Haven. I was excited and stressed, as I had no idea what to expect.

I woke up early and went out to run. I ran longer and harder than usual. I dressed in a business suit with a blouse and tie-scarf around the collar. The suit was a gray-green color. Bill had bought it for me for Christmas. It was expensive and I wanted to take it back for something more practical, but Bill said he wanted me to keep it. I was glad I did.

"Good luck, Mom. I know you can do it. You look great," as Anne kissed my cheek and left for school.

"Be careful driving," Bill said.

The class started at 8:30 a.m., and it took an hour to get to New Haven if you knew where you were going. I left Glastonbury at 7:00 a.m. to give myself lots of time to find my way. My therapist and friends had encouraged me by saying, "Work is good therapy for you." Only once on my drive did I think about Sarah. I talked to her for just a minute on my drive.

"Here I go Sarah, wish me luck. You are always with me. I love you." I spoke out loud and cried for just a minute.

Now pull yourself together, Jackie. What kind of role model are you anyway? Crying for God's sake.

I found Church Street and parked the company car in the company parking garage around the corner from Church on George Street. I walked down the street and around the corner and found the training center. I was twenty minutes early, so I walked around the block to quiet my anxiety.

I don't know what I'm doing here. Who needs it. They're probably all kids. What will they think of me? Who cares. I need it, that's who needs it. Hurry up, for God's sake, or you'll be late.

There was a security guard who directed me to the second floor conference room after I had shown him my company ID. I went up a flight of stairs and through two doors, coming face-to-face with a receptionist. She knew who I was before I said anything.

"Here's your name tag. You're Jackie, right? The classroom is the second one down on the left through that door."

She pointed to the door. I thanked her, took my name tag, and continued through the door.

The tables were in a horseshoe arrangement with a blackboard, easel, and podium at the center. I was the last person to enter the class. There were three men and two women, all veterans of the company who were transferred from management jobs. There was a camaraderie among them that I didn't share. I was also the oldest one in the room.

As I sat there, I had a steely resolve to make this a good thing.

Our main instructor for the training came into the room and introduced herself to us. Her name was JoAnn Cavallaro. She was dressed in a navy blue suit with a white blouse and a puffy little scarf around her neck. It was the standard dress for women in business at the time. It was stiff-looking, but the message was clear; she was a woman in business. She had really large horn-rimmed glasses with thick lenses. Her look was rigid, but there was a gentleness and kindness behind those glasses. I knew that I saw or felt something about her that was very special.

She turned toward the black board, picked up a piece of chalk, and wrote on the board, JOANN CAVALLARO.

"Good morning. I am JoAnn and I will be your lead trainer for the next twelve weeks. Let's get started. We'll go around the room and introduce ourselves. Tell us about who you are, what department you come from, and what you did there. Then tell us why you think this is the right program for you. I'll start and tell you a little about myself and how I have came to be here today."

JoAnn told us that she had been a high school English teacher before joining the company. She came in as an account executive and had been promoted into the training center. As she spoke, she made eye contact with everyone in the room. I could see her eyes when she looked at me and knew that underneath the cool exterior and thick glasses was a warm and sympathetic person. Her gaze lingered on me and I wondered why. Did she think I didn't belong? Was I so different from the others in the class? They seemed relaxed sitting around the table.

Get a grip. You are so damned insecure. Just let it go. You can do this.

I can't answer any of those questions, for God's sake. Who am I? Lost is who I am, and I don't really know if I do want this career path—it's a promotion, that's why I want it. And oh, by the way, I have to leave early every Tuesday for family counseling in Hartford. Is that going to be okay? Sure, sure, we'll see just how kind she is when I ask her that. Well, I'll just have to drop out if she says no.

I was the last one to talk and somehow said something that passed as sane. The company had never before had a non-management person be promoted to management and enter this class. And furthermore, they had never had anyone my age in the class. I was an anomaly. Yes, that's it, that's what I was, at least that.

I knew then that I wanted to be successful in this new job. I wanted to succeed. I sat there with my heart in a dark place and maybe that was not going to change, but I could do something for me. *It all starts with you. You can only control you, no one else.*

The first day of class was on a Wednesday, so I didn't have to ask for the time off on Tuesdays for a few days. On Friday, I asked JoAnn if I might talk to her after class. Sarah's illness was still new and, although friends and family knew about it, I had never talked to anyone outside of that circle. I was not going to tell JoAnn a long story, but I certainly owed her a serious reason for the change in schedule I needed.

"JoAnn, I have a very big request to make. I have a standing appointment with a doctor in Hartford every Tuesday afternoon at 4:00 p.m. To keep it, it I will have to leave here at 3:00 p.m. I know this is asking a lot of you and, if there was any other arrangement I could make, I would. It is for my daughter, who is not well—," I continued and my eyes began to water. I kept talking until JoAnn put her hand on my arm.

"Jackie, stop. It's all right. We'll change Tuesdays so you won't miss anything important." She looked at me through those thick glasses and I saw the kindness. She understood; somehow, she saw me.

I had never felt a connection like that before. I had many friends, but we dealt with each other through our own filters. I had always had a wall around me—the wall worked for me. I was safe behind it, but when Sarah got sick nothing stayed the same. The wall may have still been there, but I was no longer protected behind it. I didn't understand anything the same way.

The weeks of training went on. I liked all of it. Our class grew to know one another and to grow close through the long, common experience of the training. JoAnn became my mentor in subtle ways. I sensed this. I think I was a cause for her. She had great confidence in me that energized me. We ended our training with a celebration dinner party. I was proud of my accomplishment and eager to start the real job, but the real job meant leaving the security of the class and the classroom and JoAnn's caring support. What I didn't know was how much I had grown to care about JoAnn.

"We'll be in touch, don't worry, I want to make sure you are successful after all my hard work," she said.

Maria, one of my classmates, and I were assigned to the same office in Hartford.

"I'll call and we can get together for dinner," Maria said, "You, me, and Jackie."

We met for dinner at least once a month. Bill never understood why we did that.

"Don't you see enough of those people during the day? You have to go out to dinner with them, too?"

I stopped trying to explain how important the connection was to me. He didn't care. He cared only about his own needs, not mine. Andrew and Anne were both away at school, so it left just the two of us at home. Our private pain about Sarah separated us. We were split apart from the inside out. Life at home was not comfortable or happy. Much to my surprise, I was good at sales. As a matter of fact, I was the most successful salesperson in my class. My success made me feel good.

JoAnn and I were in constant communication with each other. It was not long before she and I met for dinner alone without Maria on a regular basis. I loved JoAnn and told her so. I shared more with her about myself, my family, Andrew, Anne, and Bill. I shared about Sarah and her illness, about my life, and how I was feeling. She listened carefully to everything I said.

How did this happen? How is it that a mature woman with three grown children, a house in suburbia, and a husband who worked hard and cared about his family, could find herself in a relationship with a woman?

The assumptions we all make about our lives sometimes aren't valid. When Sarah tried to kill herself, all of our assumptions about our life disappeared. This wasn't ever supposed to happen. Our world as we knew it stopped. The old routines stopped. They stopped for all of us in different ways. Questions that had never been asked or needed to be asked were there in front of us.

Who are we? Who am I? What am I doing here?

We started with family therapy. At first it was me and Bill. If Andrew or Anne was home on vacation they also joined us. Bill and I also belonged to a support group of parents at the hospital. It was humbling. I came face to face with pain, the pain of other parents.

"Sarah is not like these other kids."

"Sarah gets all A's in school. She doesn't use drugs. She doesn't act out."

"She is not sick like the other kids."

Well, yes, she is sick, very sick, as a matter of fact, sicker than most of the children in the hospital; so sick that she couldn't be left alone at all, not for a moment. It took a very long time to really understand how very sick Sarah was. Even now, twenty-five years later, time has not dulled the pain I feel when I remember those years.

Our family therapy lasted only six months. The honesty in those sessions was tough. *This is no time to be polite*, I said to myself. I felt stripped of all my protection against the world.

Frank Ahern was the therapist.

"How do you share feelings in your house?" he asked.

"We don't share," I said. Bill glared at me.

"What are you talking about, of course we share feelings."

"When was the last time we did that?" I asked.

"Oh for God's sake, Jackie, we talk all the time. We talk about how the kids are doing in school, where they should go to school, and where we should go on vacation. We talk all the time."

"That is not talking about feelings. We don't talk about feelings. As a matter of fact, if anyone heard us, they would wonder what we felt about anything. We'd never know. Do you care how any of us feel about anything?"

He glared at me again. We probably could have stopped the therapy after a month, because we never moved beyond our differences. As I let myself be honest and speak honestly, it was clear that Bill and I had two distinctly different perceptions of our family life. There was no bridging that difference.

It's easy to live a lie. That's what I had been doing. Bill wasn't living a lie. He had everything he ever wanted and said so, often. Once I began being honest, I couldn't stop. It was the fuel that gave me the energy to move and to make changes happen in my life.

My world was expanding far beyond the suburban walls of Glastonbury. I would still see my Glastonbury friends at an occasional party. There were two types of women in Glastonbury—those who worked and those who didn't. There was about a fifty-fifty split. Those who did work were teachers, teacher's aides, or nurses.

"Jackie, I haven't seen you in ages, what are you doing now?" Lee asked at one of the many traditional Christmas cocktail parties. Lee was one of my very best friends who had faded into the suburban backdrop after Sarah was hospitalized for "some mental illness." She was a reading teacher in Glastonbury.

"I'm working in sales for SNET in New Haven," I answered.

"Do you like it? You drive to New Haven every day? Isn't that a long ride? Is it worth it?"

I might as well have said Chicago for the reaction I got. Anything outside of Glastonbury was a foreign place with unknown people. Dangerous stuff. I don't remember my answer. I remember telling her how much I liked my job—dealing with different companies, the challenge of selling, and the expansiveness of the new experience.

"Bob would never let me do anything like that. He's insanely jealous," she said. "How does Bill feel about what you're doing?"

I wanted to say "I really don't give a shit!" but of course I said something just as stupid back to her like, "He's fine with it and loves the money I'm making." That got her attention.

Of course, I knew Lee was absolutely right about Bob not tolerating any job except teaching. He was jealous even if Lee and I had a conversation for too long without including him.

I was listening to Lee and for the first time I was hearing her. Hearing who she really was. I had often heard people talk about what their gut told them. I never knew what that meant until now.

The truth was that Bill was not all right with my new job. He didn't like any of it. He didn't like the person I was becoming either. Almost everything bothered him. We would socialize with dear friends, like Janet and Hank, and Bill would get enraged at my talking to Hank about sales. I could almost hear the voice in his head.

"The little woman (a.k.a. bitch) doesn't know her place anymore."

One night during dinner with Janet and Hank, Hank suggested that he and I get together for lunch the next day. Hank owned an engineering company in Glastonbury and was interested in hearing more about a new telephone system for his plant.

"No, Jackie can't do that tomorrow; we have a family therapy appointment at the Institute," Bill answered.

I don't know how I held myself back from reacting. I was dumbstruck and outraged that Bill answered for me.

"Call me tomorrow, Jackie, and we can set up another day for the appointment," Hank said. He knew what was going on and wanted out of the conversation as soon as possible.

It was not a pretty picture that night in our house. It was the first big blow up we had. It was the first of many. At family therapy the next day we talked about what had happened the night before. I can't remember the therapist's name. It was Ed "something." Ed that suggested we begin some marriage counseling and gave us the name of someone to contact.

"That's all I need," I thought, *"another therapy/counseling/group thing. Bill won't have to worry about my job. I won't have one with all the time off I have to take."* Another suggestion Ed had for us was that we go out on dates with each other. We were to set special times to be alone together and talk, to get reacquainted. Bill loved that idea. He went into a planning mode, which was one of his favorite things to do.

We had only two dates. The first one was to meet after work for drinks and dinner at a new place in Glastonbury. Bill was there before I was and had already had at least one martini. He was pissed at having to wait for me. A very nice start to the date. I had a drink. We both tried hard to make civil conversation. I tried hard to stay away from work subjects, but when he asked what I had done that day, of course I told him. I know I came alive when I talked about it. I could see Bill getting annoyed. He was not a subtle man.

"By the way," he interrupted, "Someone from your office called when I was home, a guy by the name of Jimmie Rogers. He wants you to pick him up tomorrow morning on West Service Road. What's going on here anyway? Why does he need a ride from *you* and what is he doing calling you at home?"

"We're going to call on a customer tomorrow. It just makes sense to go together."

"Well, I don't like it. I don't like any of it! Who the hell do you think you are anyway? You and the fucking phone company!" His voice was getting louder and louder.

"Bill, I am going to leave right now if you don't stop." I knew he wouldn't, because the martinis had kicked in. I had seen this before.

"Yeah, sure, go ahead Mrs. Smartass, but not before you pay your part of the bill here. You and the fuckin' phone company!"

I got up from the table and left him there. He must have paid the bill and he probably had another drink before he left. I didn't care what he did. I did know that he would be wild when he came home. I decided that I could not sleep in the same bed with him that night and moved into Sarah's room.

Chapter 28

Parallel Paths

Dr. Boynton never told us what Sarah's illness was; that is, she never labeled it. If she did, we didn't hear it. Recently, while cleaning out an accumulation of papers, letters, and pictures, I came across an essay that Sarah wrote when she was a senior at the Institute of Living High School in 1983. She was seventeen and applying to Hartford College for Women. The essay was part of the application. It is written in very careful longhand on lined paper. Page three of the essay reads:

"The most significant event in my life has been my painful psychiatric hospitalization. At the age of thirteen, I was admitted to the Adolescent Psychiatric Unit at Mount Sinai Hospital in Hartford. I am now seventeen and have been at the Institute of Living since the age of fourteen.

My emotional breakdown was caused basically by the lack of individuality and freedom of expression I felt as a child. Although I continued to function well in school, I entered a deep depression and became numb to my feelings. As I was operating under a great deal of pressure, I eventually lost touch with myself, my family, and my world. The task of learning how to identify, express, and deal with my emotions has been very painful, difficult, and strenuous. However, today I feel stronger and happier than I ever imagined was possible at my young age. The members of my family have grown emotionally along with me, and have given me their undying support and love."

It sounds so simple, almost benign. It was not. It occurred to me as I read and re-read Sarah's essay that some of my journey was not unlike hers. I found myself gradually undoing all that was wrong or ill-fitting in my life. I, too, was learning "how to identify, express and deal with my emotions."

Almost everything was wrong. I didn't know what I was going to find as I opened my heart and my mind to the world around me. I had spent the first part of my life doing what I was supposed to do without thinking about what I wanted to do. There really was not much of an "I" to know. I was programmed. I never even picked out my own clothes. My mother did that for me. Bill took over the job from my mother. Of course, I colluded in all of this, I never said "no" or "leave me alone." In many ways, I married my mother. I had a hard shell around me to protect me. No one was getting close. It protected me just fine, which was unlike Sarah who had no shell around her. She was sensitive and vulnerable. I was closed off to anything that would hurt me.

Once the hard shell cracked, honest feelings were exposed. There was no turning back after that. Bill didn't know who I was or what I was talking about. When the divorce papers were served to him, he was shocked.

"What the hell is the matter with you? What do you want anyway? You have a nice house and a good life. What more do you want?"

He had everything he wanted, so it never occurred to him that maybe the kids and I didn't have everything we wanted. It was Bill's world.

Sarah needed distance from all of us so that she could find herself. She needed structure in her life to bring order back where there was only noise and chaos. To this day, Sarah lives away from us and it works for her. She needs the distance so she can be her own person.

I needed to leave Bill to be my own person. I married him for all the wrong reasons. It was not enough for me to finally say that to myself; I had to tell him, too. There was nothing else that I could say that would make him understand the divorce better than that. There was no way for me to be my own person in the marriage. And, saying it was liberating.

"You bitch. How can you say that to me after all these years?" he said one night after having a few martinis. It was the hurt that cut the deepest and because of it, the divorce took on a passion and intensity that knew no bounds.

When I first met with my lawyer about the divorce he said, "This is an easy one—no minor children, no complex financials, and a fifty-fifty split. This will only cost you about $2,500.00." Well, he was off by a factor of more than ten. The divorce cost me more than $27,000.00. And if I hadn't said, "I quit. You win," it would have cost me much more. Even after the final decision, Bill was going to appeal. He punished me the only way he could—by not giving me the money the court ordered him to give me.

"You're such a smartass. Let's see just how smart you are. You think it's easy earning a living. Go right ahead, smartass."

I paid dearly, but it was worth it. It was like paying to get out of prison. Like Sarah, I had to find out who I was. Who was I without Bill, without our house on Carriage Drive? I had to learn that I was a separate person. I had to learn to take myself seriously. I had to learn that I made a difference in my world. Cutting the ties of a marriage doesn't happen with the final divorce papers. That's the beginning. I cringed at the sound of Bill's voice for years.

We'll never know the hell that Sarah went through in the early years at the Institute of Living. We knew only what was shared and what we saw. We saw burn marks on her arms from where she put out her cigarettes. We know she was confined on more than one occasion in a safe room with padded walls. We know that she had to be put in a straight jacket and submerged in cold water to calm her. These are the things that we know. We don't know what hell she endured in her mind.

On the outside, after the worst was over, we saw a new Sarah. We saw the Sarah who smoked cigarettes and wore lots and lots of makeup. We saw the Sarah who had six or seven holes in each ear for various earrings. We saw the Sarah with multi-layered clothes: a skirt, long pants, tights, a shirt, a sweater and a shawl worn all at once. We saw Sarah the vegetarian. She was working her way to find herself.

By 1983 Sarah started her new life at Hartford College. In 1984 she transferred to Emerson College in Boston and graduated with high honors in 1986. Bill sent me copies of the tuition bills every semester so that I could pay half. He never let up. But I too, like Sarah, was having some success. I was learning and growing and finding myself.

Chapter 29

Running Away

I know I was running away. I was running from the pain. I was running from my life in Glastonbury.

I set my alarm for 5:30 every morning to go out and run in the dark. I ran for about a half hour. Our house was quiet. Andrew was away at Gettysburg College and Anne was finishing high school soon to go away to Rhode Island School of Design in Providence, Rhode Island. Running helped me quiet the frenzied energy I had. Moving my body stopped the ache.

I continued to do some of the social things I had done for years. I played bridge with a group once a month; I belonged to a birthday group that celebrated the birthdays of six friends; and I played tennis once a week at Pine Brook Swim and Tennis club—outdoors in the summer and indoors in the winter. None of that was fun anymore. I said the same things and laughed at the right places, but I didn't care about any of that. Slowly, I stopped going to the bridge group. I also backed out of tennis and began to miss some of the birthday celebrations.

Some of my friends sent me notes of concern about Sarah. Some friends asked me how I was and others said nothing. I understood the discomfort around me. I didn't mind because I was too far away in my head to care.

I have seen pictures of myself during that time, and the sadness on my face is painful to see. Anne did an oil painting of me during those early times of Sarah's illness. I have it in the hall closet. I can't throw it away, but I can't hang it up either. She did a calligraphy piece that she gave me with the oil painting.

For Mom
The Pine is Brave
That Changes Not its Color
Bearing the Snow
People Too
Like it Should Be
      —*Tanka: Emperor Hiroheto*

I've kept that hanging in my office. It's been thirty years since Sarah got sick. It's taken that long for me to look back and really see it.

I wasn't running away from Anne or Andrew. My heart was heavy with pain for all of us. Somehow we all turned inward, away from each other. We had to be private to live through the time.

Anne was a very good student, captain of the tennis team, captain of the basketball team, and an artist with considerable talent. *How wonderful for her*, I would think. We tried to get to all of her tennis matches and basketball games. She seemed to be doing everything just right. She was accepted at Rhode Island School of Design. It was her first choice and she heard early in the year, so she could relax about her plans for the fall. I thought, *Good, I don't have to worry about Anne.*

I do remember worrying about her diet. She didn't eat very much. She'd also started to run. She ran every day for five or six miles. She lost weight.

"She'll be all right, Jackie. Leave her alone." Bill would say.

Anne was talking to a therapist every week. She liked the woman and looked forward to the sessions with her.

It was the spring of Anne's senior year that I was promoted at SNET and began the twelve week training program in New Haven. I was working very long hours and spent most nights doing homework for my training. We had one week of final tests, which included a videotaping of a sales call. This was a pass/fail test. If the panel didn't like your role play, you were out of the program. It was Thursday night at 10:00 p.m. and my videotaping was Friday morning.

"Mom, can I talk to you?" Anne called through the den door.

"Come on in, Anne. I'm working on my role play for my videotaping tomorrow. Can it wait until tomorrow night?"

"No, Mom, I have to tell you something."

"I am a wreck about this, Anne. Please, can't it wait? Why didn't you tell me early in the evening? Well, all right, come in and sit down."

"Mom, I think I'm a lesbian."

She must have agonized over telling me. She must have had long and sleepless nights thinking about what her sexuality would mean to her. What would we think? What about her friends?

I was shocked, but the timing and the way she said it gave the moment an unreal quality. I wish I had hugged her and told her I loved her, but I didn't. I didn't know what to do or say.

"You're so young Anne, don't close off your options. You have so much living to do."

That is what I said. It sounds so cold now when I think about it. We talked a little more. I asked if she had told her therapist. She had. Her therapist suggested that she tell me. She didn't care if I told her father or not, but she was going to tell Andrew when he came home for vacation. I did hug her when we had no more to say. That was the end of my studying. I felt upset at just about everything. I was angry that Anne would have chosen that moment to share such big news with me. I was angry that she was a lesbian. I was nervous about the test. I was angry with myself for my reaction to Anne. It felt like an intrusion and I resented it. There was a new selfishness I had, and I didn't like how I felt in those shoes.

I am not proud of that moment.

Chapter 30

Old Friends

Sarah's illness shook our world with such intensity that it seemed everything we believed in had been shattered like glass and would never be put back together the same way. This included our values, our beliefs, our sense of right and wrong—our very core. We didn't know it then, but there would be no going back. When your own smooth cocoon cracks, the exposed inside is not smooth. The old cocoon is gone and re-bonding is not possible.

Our marriage slowly broke. We had been together twenty-two years. We had buried feelings and sacrificed intimacy for those twenty-two years. We were wide open now and it was time to dig ourselves out. At first, our concern and care for Sarah took all of our energy; we lost ourselves in our focus on her. It was one small insight after another that led me down a new path. It was not so much a change, but an uncovering of buried truths about ourselves that made it feel like a change. Simply put, I felt that we had been living a lie.

In fairness to Bill, he never thought he was living a lie. He had everything he wanted in the marriage. He said that many times. He also said he loved me many times. I never felt the love. There can be a disconnection between the words and the feeling. Unspoken communication is always far stronger than any words. I never let myself think about that; I think it was part of my denial.

After I married, I gradually lost contact with almost all of my friends from my single days. Bill didn't like most of them, so it was easier to let go and build a new life with new friends we could share. My old friends would have been a reminder to me of who I was and that would not be good for the marriage.

As time passed and old friends learned about what was happening in my life, I began to hear from them. First, Joan called. She had been a very dear friend for years. She and her husband Bob had gone to Colby College with my brother Bill. They lived in Lynnfield, Massachusetts and I lived in Glastonbury, Connecticut so we decided to meet for lunch in Sturbridge, Massachusetts. I hadn't seen Joan for at least fifteen years except for two family weddings where we spoke only briefly. I knew then that she was trying to reach out, but I wasn't ready to let my guard down. I remember feeling so nervous that I almost called and cancelled.

I was early and she was late. I was sitting in the lobby of the Sheraton Hotel pretending to read a magazine when Joan tapped me on the shoulder.

"Jackie, how great to see you!" I stood up and we hugged each other.

"Oh, Joan, it's been so long—too long." I had a lump in my throat that I was trying to hide. Tears had become a big part of my life since Sarah's illness began. I had to work hard at not just blurting out fifteen years of history to her along with an apology for neglecting our friendship.

We talked about light things at first. Joan had two teenage sons who she talked about, as well as about Bob's teaching and writing and about her own career in education.

"Now, how about you?"

"Oh, I'm okay," I choked out.

"Well, honestly, Jackie, you don't look okay. Billy told me about Sarah. But you, Jackie, what about you?"

It wasn't long before I felt comfortable enough to talk honestly to Joan. I remember feeling the best I had felt in many months. It felt wonderful to talk truthfully about everything. The warmth and comfort of being with someone who cared about me no matter what, was overwhelming. It was the beginning of letting myself feel something, letting the wall crack a little, and feeling safe enough to be vulnerable. I felt a profound misery and exhaustion, but I also felt alive and strangely energized at the same time.

I learned that none of my old friends liked Bill. They wondered why I would marry him. To them, the pieces never fit. I think I knew this, but could never let myself think about it.

Many times since that day Joan has said to me, "I'm mad at myself for not saying anything to you about Bill. I just watched—we all just stood by and let you do it." The truth is that even if she had said, "I don't like him, or don't do it," there is no way I would or could have heard it.

My friend Gretchen called shortly after I first met with Joan. Gretchen had been a classmate at Connecticut College and a bridesmaid in my wedding. She was another friend that Bill didn't like. Gretchen married a few months before we did and had her first baby a few months later. It was not until years later that I realized why Bill didn't like Gretchen. She was pregnant before she married. She also had the audacity to nurse her baby in our living room the one time she visited us with the baby. Bill was defined by his rules. Like so much else between us, he kept those rules secret until after we married.

Gretchen and I made plans to meet in Providence, Rhode Island. Anne was at Rhode Island School of Design, and I was going to visit her for lunch and see some new piece of sculpture she had just finished. Gretchen drove from Boston to meet me for dinner.

Bill was home alone. He didn't like any of this. Although I wasn't thinking about divorce at the time, I knew Bill was nervous about my new independence. This particular Saturday was a turning point in some way.

Anne and I had a wonderful time together that day. She had been so caring of me through the early time of Sarah's illness. We had lunch and went to a new student exhibition. The sculpture Anne had on exhibition was one she had done of me from a picture she had taken of me just after Sarah went to the Institute. Such an incredibly sad woman. Was that me? I cried tears of joy and sadness.

Later on, Gretchen and I met at a small restaurant on Benefit Street called Panache. We met there many times after that. Gretchen hugged me hard and I cried again. *What would I have done without these special people in my life?* I thought. I still think that to this day. We stayed at Panache until it closed. I called Bill at about 9:00 p.m. to say I would be late. He was not happy. I remember I told Gretchen that he was pissed. She said, as only she could, "Fuck him!"

Bill and Gretchen didn't like each other at all. It was no surprise he didn't want me spending so much time with her, and her "Fuck him," was said with more than usual force. I felt somehow empowered by doing what I wanted to do. I wanted to be in Providence with my friend. I didn't care about what he wanted at all.

That night before I left Panache, I called Bill again to say I would be on my way. It was 11:00 p.m. This meant I wouldn't get home until after 1:00 a.m. He was furious with me.

"What are you doing? Who do you think you are keeping me waiting all day and all night? That's the last time you'll do this to me!" Blah, blah, blah!!!

I remember hanging up the phone and thinking, *Who does he think he is, I'll do what ever I want, whenever I want! Gretchen is right fuck him!!*

Chapter 31

Dinner

I began to bury myself in my work. Work was the place where I could break loose. I was completely energized there. I was moving from dark to light, and the light gave me a strength I never had before. In some ways, Sarah and I were moving on a parallel path. For five years we traveled fast through a new world and both came out different people in the end. Both of us were not just different people but healthier and more whole than when we started out.

Bill was changing too, but not like me. He had not been in a shell and so there was no cracking open for him. He began to blame the "fucking phone company" for our failing marriage.

I knew that Bill would not like any of my work friends. He didn't like anyone who was just my friend. But I decided that I'd invite some of my class for dinner after we had completed our training. JoAnn was invited. He thought that was a good idea, because he wanted to meet these people that I was so engaged with. It was summer and we would have drinks and dinner on the porch. The porch was large and screened in on three sides looking out over the grass and woods. There were spotlights in the yard that made the trees look thick and black. The porch had a large glass table and wrought iron chairs. There were four wrought iron armchairs and a couch. It was my favorite place in the house in the summer.

Bill was territorial about "his" house. That is, he was the boss of all things in the house. He made the drinks, he decided when we would eat, and he led the conversation. Maria and her husband Rick, Bob Franco and his wife Judy, and JoAnn were the guests.

"Jackie," I heard him call, "Would you bring some napkins out here?" The evening was filled with Bill calling me, directing me, or correcting me. He was showing them all that he was the man of the house.

"Rick," JoAnn asked, "What kind of marketing do you do for your financial planning business?"

"Oh, you're a financial planner," Bill repeated. "I'd like to know just what kind of commission structure you guys work under. You get paid to push certain stocks, don't you?" It was a definitely a challenging question.

"Well, no, not exactly," Rick started to answer.

"Oh, come on now. I know all about how you guys work. You don't do it for nothing," Bill interrupted.

There was an increasing tension on the porch. Al just watched and listened. JoAnn tried to change the subject. I kept moving, thinking to myself what a stupid idea this dinner party was. I know what Bill can be like; he's brave and bold on his own turf after having two martinis.

Maria came into the kitchen to help but I think it was just to get away from what was getting increasingly uncomfortable on the porch.

"Jackie, would you bring the shaker of martinis in here?"

"That's all we need," I said.

"Don't bring it in," Maria said.

Bill was doing most of the drinking. JoAnn was sipping a glass of red wine and Al and his wife were having cranberry juice.

A few minutes passed and again we heard, "Jackie, where are those martinis?"

JoAnn came into the kitchen and said, "You'd better give me the shaker. He's getting angry, but I swear I can't figure out why."

"Oh God, you guys, I am so sorry things are turning out this way. Are Al and Judy all right out there?"

"They're fine, Jackie, don't worry about them. You know Al. He's easy."

"I'm going to get the dinner on the table before he can finish his next drink. You two go in there and try to change the subject," I said.

Hurry do it fast. Get it done, over. Get them out. What made me think I could do this and have it be okay? Nothing was okay here anymore. I should have known Bill would try to show off. He thinks he knows so much. Listen to him out there; they're talking about the telephone business and he's talking like he knows more than they do. What an asshole. I am so embarrassed. I can't imagine what my friends are thinking about me and Bill. What does it say about me that I am married to this man? I know what is says. I know very well what it says. Who was that woman who married Bill? Not me, not anymore.

Even a change in subject didn't change Bill's aggressive behavior. JoAnn tried to talk about sales and the sales training. Bill knew all about that, too.

"Salesmen, they're all the same. Can't trust them. If you know what you want you don't need a salesman to sell it to you."

It was a showstopper and thank God no one answered him. As a matter of fact, everything Bill said from then on that evening was a showstopper. There was no conversation, just dictums from Bill.

I served the dinner of salad and chicken with pesto over pasta. I remember what it was, but I don't remember one thing about eating it or how it tasted. I just wanted the evening to end and have everyone leave. I served a dessert of fruit with sorbet, but no coffee. I remember thinking, *I can't serve coffee, they'll linger.* I had to get them out as fast as possible.

What will they think of me after tonight? Can I show myself at work tomorrow? My fault. Stupid, stupid me. I should have known not to have this dinner party. It has never worked for my friends or acquaintances to be welcomed by him. We can only have his friends or our friends, not my friends. I can't have friends on my own without him. After all, it's his life that matters, not mine.

Finally, Rick stood up and said that it was time he and Maria headed home. Al, Judy, and JoAnn stood up, too.

"Thanks, so much, Jackie and Bill. Nice to meet you Bill," Maria said.

"Nice to meet you Bill," Rick said and put out his hand. Bill didn't see it or didn't want to shake it.

I tried not to see Bill. I was saying good-bye and ushering everyone out to the driveway. I followed and shut the door. I could hear Bill going up the stairs to bed.

I hugged each person good-bye. I felt empty inside. I tried to see some reaction to the evening on their faces. I didn't see anything. *Oh, God, what a mess*, I thought.

I was alone cleaning up the dinner dishes. I took a long time. I felt like I was moving in slow motion around the house from the porch to the kitchen, loading the dishwasher and wiping the counters. I knew Bill was asleep, I could hear him snoring, but I didn't want to go to bed. I just couldn't go up there like everything was fine. It wasn't fine at all. I sat down on the porch in the dark looking out at the woods. I stayed there all night.

Chapter 32

JoAnn

Some things are so big, so beyond everyday experiences that they can't be understood right away. The changes and feelings come in waves that hold us for the moment, then recede. They are too much for us to handle or cope with all at once. Meeting JoAnn was like that for me, although I didn't know that at first. I knew I liked and admired her from the first day I met her. I felt a connection with her. She looked at me as if she knew me, knew me inside, knew me better than I knew myself. When she looked at me, I felt safe and warm and frightened all at once. At that moment, I didn't know myself at all. I was looking for me. I was lost.

Sarah's illness stopped our lives and shook our balance so much that the old routines, the everyday sameness was gone. I was starting over with new rules that had not yet been defined.

JoAnn listened to me. This may not sound profound, but for me it was. No one had ever really listened to me. My mother never listened to me and Bill never listened to me. I didn't know what it would feel like to be heard. I know I played a role in all of this, because it does take two. I didn't like not being heard, but it was part of who I was now—a backdrop, a "pretend" person. I was a good actor so most people didn't know this about me. I had a strong front that masked my identity.

But in class, with JoAnn, I made a difference, I mattered. It was slow to take hold. I was slow to feel the difference, but it was powerful stuff when it began to work. The twelve weeks of training was just the beginning and it was not easy. I was filled with self-doubt. JoAnn saw that and cared enough to work with me to change. She saw that I could not just do the work, but that I would excel in the work.

I had to tell JoAnn about Sarah, because on Tuesdays I had to leave class early to go to family therapy. She listened closely and sympathetically, but asked no questions. As the weeks went by, I grew more and more drawn to JoAnn—not overtly, but I would feel myself get excited as I drove each day to New Haven, eager to get to class or maybe even see her for a few minutes before class in her office. She was always business-like, but always ready to listen. I could see caring in her eyes behind the big glasses she wore.

The twelve-week training ended. We had a farewell dinner on the last Friday to celebrate the completion of our training. I was glad to have completed the training and to have received a good evaluation letter to start my new job, but I was not happy about leaving the comfort and security of JoAnn's classroom.

I had one too many martinis and became somewhat sloppy in my farewell. I read a poem that I wrote about the class and JoAnn and the twelve weeks. Everyone laughed and enjoyed it.

I guess I read that all right., They're laughing. Are they laughing at the poem or me? JoAnn is laughing too. She would never laugh at me. It must be funny. I think they like me. Maria likes me. Maybe I should sit down. Yes, sit down. They all want copies of the poem so they must like it. I'll read it again. No, I'd better sit down. I think I should go home.

"Maria, maybe you could drive Jackie home in the company car." JoAnn said.

I think she was whispering or maybe not. Everyone is getting up to go. Their lips are moving, but no words are coming out. I don't hear them. I should get going, too. Where's my poem?, Where's my pocketbook? Oh, Maria has it and JoAnn has the poem. She must have liked it, I thought she would, I hoped she would. I like her so much. Stop, stop, right now. Don't you dare cry. Stupid ass.

"Jackie, Maria is going to drive you home. Are you all set to go?"

Am I all set to go? Me, all set to go? God, of course not. I just got into everything here and now I have to go? Go home?, Go home to what? Where did everyone go? I guess I said goodbye, I hope I did. "Yes, I'm all set." What else can I say? Everyone else is gone. I'm not going to stay here alone.

"Let's walk out to the car together. That was a funny poem you wrote, Jackie. Thanks—I liked it even though you did poke a little fun at me."

I did? Oh yes, I guess I did, but it's because I like you so much. Do you know that?, Oh, of course you know that, you with your knowing eyes looking right into me. Am I talking out loud or am I just thinking this? Nobody's looking at me so I guess I'm talking to myself.

"I want to keep tabs on all of you, so I'll be arranging dinners with you over the next few weeks. Maria and Jackie, I'll be in touch. Since you're both in Hartford, maybe we can meet halfway someplace."

I'm in the car, whew. The window is open. I need some air. JoAnn has her hand on my shoulder. That's nice. What is she doing? She has her hand on my head. She's saying something I can't hear. Maybe that's a good thing. I'll just smile at her. Maria is talking to her about me. She'll take me home.

Maria, sweet Maria, stopped for coffee and drove me home. I was more or less coherent by the time we reached Glastonbury. Bill was sleeping and woke only to grunt about how late I was. The martinis numbed me. It was the coward's way out. Over the next months, Maria and JoAnn and I had regular dinners together to talk about business. We eventually talked less and less about business and more and more about everything else. Maria was now living in Longmeadow, Massachusetts with her new husband, Rick, so eventually she declined the dinners. That left JoAnn and me alone. There was no real business reason for JoAnn to meet with me. I didn't need any more coaching, training, or encouragement. As a matter of fact, I was doing very well selling—it seems I was the best salesperson in our class. But, we continued to meet, more often and for longer periods of time. JoAnn would sometimes bring a book or poem or essay that she wanted to share with me. She would read it to me and we would talk about it. She never stopped being the former English teacher. JoAnn had been promoted from the training center to a marketing job.

We spoke on the phone every day, sometimes more than once. I trusted her more than I had ever trusted anyone. Slowly, I relaxed and let her know me. I felt safe. I realized that I had never let anyone know me. I was guarded and afraid, afraid to be vulnerable and afraid to be hurt. In some ways, JoAnn was the first person in my life to want to know me. She shared herself with me, too. I saw her insecurities, too, although very different from mine. They were hiding behind her personal power and intellect.

It took many months for me to know that this was love. What else could it be—friendship, infatuation? I didn't know what love was. I had never been in love before JoAnn. This was tough stuff to hold on to. I fought with it over those many months, just like those waves of feelings that overwhelm and then fade. But there was no going back behind the walls that I had knocked down. My feelings were out in the open and to cover them up would be to suffocate.

Chapter 33

Secrets

In the spring of 1982, JoAnn and I planned an overnight trip to visit Anne in Providence. She was a sophomore at Rhode Island School of Design (RISD). I had driven to Providence many times for a day, but never an overnight. Bill was always fine with visits to the kids, and even the overnight didn't bother him. He didn't know that JoAnn was visiting Anne with me. We left New Haven at 4:00 p.m. on Friday and arrived at the Hilton Hotel at 6:00 p.m. Anne had made dinner reservations for 7:30 p.m. at Panache, one of Providence's new restaurants. We checked in to the hotel and drove to Anne's apartment on Benefit Street. Benefit Street has gaslights and cobblestone streets with brick sidewalks. The houses are old and beautiful; at least they are on the outside. Those that rented to students had the sloppy worn look that comes with year after year of wear. JoAnn was a little nervous. She had met Anne just once before. I noticed her nervousness, but said nothing about it.

Anne was happy to see us and show us what she'd done to the apartment. In her four years at RISD, this Benefit Street apartment was the nicest one she had. I could see that Anne was focused on JoAnn. I imagined she was thinking, *Who is she? Why is she such a close friend of my mother's?*

We walked down Benefit Street. Anne took us through the RISD art museum and showed us some of the workshops where she spent most of her time. This was Anne's special place and she knew it well. Her world of art was so different from my world. I loved seeing her and hearing her talk about what she did and how she did it.

We walked to the restaurant. We had a drink. JoAnn asked Anne questions about her artwork. Those were easy questions for Anne. She was most animated when she talked about her work.

"How is it that you know my mom so well?" Anne asked.

"She was in my training class for twelve weeks. We've spent a lot of time together. She's told me all about you and how talented you are. When she asked if I wanted to visit you I said, 'sure' and here I am," JoAnn answered.

Anne took my hand and held it for a minute, then she put her arm around me and gave me a little sideways hug at the table.

"Have you met my father?" Anne asked.

"Just once when your mom invited the class to your house for dinner. What a great house you have," JoAnn said.

There was a silence. Anne looked at me but said nothing. I knew that Anne still had questions about JoAnn, but there were not going to be any answers for her that night.

When dinner was over, we walked back to Anne's apartment and said goodbye. We were going to leave early the next morning, so we would not see Anne the next day.

"I love you, Mom," Anne said when she hugged me.

"I love you too, Anne."

"Nice to meet you, JoAnn. Don't believe everything my mother tells you about us. She exaggerates everything."

We laughed just a little and began our walk to the car.

"She's crazy about you, Jackie. I can see it in her eyes when she looks at you. How great that is," JoAnn said.

"She has always been close to me in a very strong and different way. I guess I've told you that when she was just four or five and Bill would ask me for something at dinner, Anne would answer for me. Something like, 'Get it yourself, Dad, Mom's not your slave.' I never knew where that was coming from."

We got back to the hotel. It was late, about midnight. This was a new experience for me, staying in a hotel with someone other than Bill. I was modest and shy about being there. JoAnn was more comfortable. She teased me about it. I changed in the bathroom into some pajamas I brought. I washed my face and brushed my teeth. JoAnn used the bathroom and came out into the bedroom. There were two double beds in the room and a TV. I turned the TV on and looked for something to watch. There was nothing on as usual, so I shut it off.

"I'm tired. Aren't you?" I asked.

"Yes, I am. But would you like a little back rub to relax? I'm pretty good at it," JoAnn said.

"Thanks, that sounds good," I answered. She came over to my bed and sat down.

I was on my stomach. She raised my top and began to rub my back. I was tense at first. I could feel my muscles tighten as JoAnn ran her hands over them. She moved her hands from my neck down to my waist, then back to my neck and over my shoulders and then further down below my waist. It was a timeless moment. I felt heat from her hands. I felt love from her hands. I could feel myself responding to her touch.

What is happening to me? Does she know what she's doing to me? Do I know what I'm doing? Don't stop. Yes, stop.

I turned around and pulled my pajama top down. I was enjoying it too much.

"I can't do this. Maybe we shouldn't be friends anymore. Maybe we shouldn't see each other anymore," I blubbered and stuttered not knowing what to do or say.

I could see the hurt on JoAnn's face. She was embarrassed. She loved me and I loved her. Wasn't that enough?

We talked for a long time in the dark. I was certain that night that I didn't want to go where the evening was taking me. My life was stamped out for me. I knew what my job was and what lay ahead.

The ride home was a somber one. I ached inside thinking about not spending time with JoAnn. JoAnn was subdued. The personal power she had was quieted by the reality we faced. I dropped her off in Guilford, holding her hand for just a moment. I cried all the way home.

The next week felt empty. Although I talked to JoAnn on the phone, I missed her. I was confused. Was I a lesbian? No, of course not, I just loved JoAnn. But that is what it's all about, a woman loving a woman. I thought, *Yes, you are a lesbian if you love JoAnn. But I only love her. I don't love all women. How could I be a lesbian? I'm married and have three children.*

I thought about nothing else for the next few weeks. JoAnn had her own pain coming to terms with her own relationship and what was happening. She asked me if I would get the name of a therapist in New Haven from my doctor. I had been in therapy for two years, ever since

Sarah had entered the Institute of Living in Hartford. JoAnn began therapy a few weeks later. I really tried to end the yearning for JoAnn, but I couldn't. JoAnn, too, was trying to put her life back where it was before she met me. There was no turning back. Life could not be the same for either one of us.

June 4, 1982 was a Monday. I know this because it marked the first day of my new life. The day started like any other. I went to my office in Hartford for the morning, and in the afternoon I drove to New Haven. Our sales team was having a meeting at the New Haven Country Club. JoAnn was a participant in the meeting. We had these meetings fairly regularly, where we heard sales results. Awards were made for high-achieving salespeople. We heard about new strategies and new changes in procedures. It was an opportunity for the salespeople to get together and reconnect, because the job was a lonely one most of the time.

It was a beautiful, warm, sunny day that reminded us that the long summer was in front of us. JoAnn asked me to have dinner with her at her house in Guilford after the meeting. I'd never been to her house and was excited to be spending the evening with her. The sales meetings always ended with a social hour of drinking. I had a martini, only one. I knew I would probably have more to drink at JoAnn's and Glastonbury was at least an hour's ride from Guilford. I had to pace myself. I loved the camaraderie at the cocktail hour—the sense of fun, the good-natured kidding, the teasing, and the story telling. Most of my co-workers were young men, but they treated me like one of their own. They said I was a "with it" woman. I liked that.

"Jackie, let's get going. Get your car and meet me at the exit of the parking lot. You'll have to follow me. Are you all set?"

"Let me just say goodbye to Jimmy Rogers. I'll be right behind you." Jimmy Rogers was our division boss and saying good bye was the politically correct thing to do. It was all a very ordinary time.

I followed JoAnn on Route 95 to Guilford. I had never been to Guilford before, but had often heard about what a nice community it was. It was like Glastonbury, but on Long Island Sound. JoAnn's house was off Jefferson Drive, down a private driveway that had only two small houses on it. It was secluded and cool, surrounded by pine trees. There was a small, circular driveway in front of the house. It was a ranch house that had a log cabin feel to it. It was cool and looked and smelled clean inside. The house was dark, the shades were drawn, and the tall pines kept the sun away. JoAnn gave me a quick tour of the house.

"This is my bedroom, this is the den, and this is Susan's room."

"Who's Susan?" I asked, JoAnn had never mentioned her before.

"Oh, she's my housemate."

I had never heard of Susan and I had never heard the term housemate.

"Where is she? Is she having dinner with us?"

"No, she's away on a business trip for a few days. She works for the company too, in marketing."

I was surprised to hear about Susan. *What is a housemate anyway? I've heard of roommate and classmate, but housemate? Why didn't she tell me about her housemate before? Is it a secret? Why would it be a secret?* I did wonder at it, but my attraction to JoAnn dimmed most other thoughts.

"You never told me that you lived with anyone. What's the big secret anyway?" I said.

"I was afraid you wouldn't understand."

"What do you mean, understand? Understand what?" I didn't have a clue what she was talking about.

JoAnn looked at me with an expression I had never seen before. Her face turned pink and then red. I hated the way she looked. It made me feel out of place and uncomfortable. I had never felt that way before with JoAnn.

"I was afraid you would run away from me."

I sat down on the couch in the den. I thought I understood. Housemate was another word for lover or lesbian.

I had never thought about lesbians before. That is, they were people I knew existed, but they were not part of my life. I read about them once in a while in books, but it was distant and didn't make a difference to me in my life at all. Here I was now, the dearest person I knew in front of me, a lesbian.

Well, so what, what does that mean to me? I love JoAnn. That doesn't make me a lesbian, does it? Or is that what this all about? I am a woman and I love a woman therefore . . . no, no that can't be right.

"Jackie, are you all right?" I was lost in my head with what I now knew about JoAnn.

"Yes, I'm fine—unsettled maybe. Yes, that's it, unsettled."

Actually, I was afraid. I don't know what frightened me. Was it just because I knew that JoAnn was a lesbian? She wasn't any different from the moment before. I had never known a lesbian before—or if did, I didn't know it. I still loved her but I might be afraid of her. Or maybe I'm afraid of me. Yes, that's it, I'm afraid of me with JoAnn.

"Tell me what you're thinking," she said and took my hand.

"I don't know what I'm thinking. Everything and nothing at the same time; junk in my head." She squeezed my hand.

Oh, God, I do love her. My body shivered with excitement.

"Come with me and let's sit outside, have a glass of wine, and relax." She led me through the kitchen.

Off the dining area, in the back of the house was a deck; that's where we sat. The deck was sunny, not cool or hot, but just right. JoAnn offered me a glass of red wine and I took it. She brought out some oysters on the half shell and her own glass of wine. We talked about the meeting and the politics at work. I drank the wine. I held JoAnn's hand softly and thanked her for inviting me for dinner. She poured me another glass of wine and we ate the oysters. She got up to check the sauce she was making and as she passed my chair, leaned over and kissed my head. I raised my face and she kissed me on the lips. I kissed her and she sat on my lap. I stopped thinking about everything. I simply loved the moment.

We kissed and hugged for what seemed like a very long time. It was dark now and I knew I had to get going. It was too late to eat dinner.

"I have to go now," I said, and I stood up. I felt wild with excitement and confused by how I felt. *I love JoAnn, and so this is okay. There is nothing wrong with kissing someone you love.* I could see that JoAnn was flustered. I had never seen her unsure of herself and it made me feel even more confused.

"Don't go. I'll get the dinner together in just a few minutes. Please. It's too foggy to drive. Stay here tonight."

"No, I have to go. Bill will be waiting for me. I'm sorry. I'll call you tomorrow."

I took my briefcase and pulled out the keys to the car. I gave JoAnn and quick hug and went out to my car. I drove around the circle and out.

Oh God, what am I doing? Look at this weather. It's so foggy I can't see anything. I can't drive in this.

I kept going. I found my way to Route 95 and the entrance to the toll road. I looked at the clock on the dash. It was 9:50 p.m. It would take me more than an hour to get home in this fog.

Who are you kidding? You know you can drive in this. But you've driven in much worse before.

I knew somewhere deep inside that this was far more than a driving decision. It was a break in the straight line of my life. I thought, *Oh, fuck, I'm turning around.*

And I turned around and went back to Jefferson Drive.

I pulled into the circular drive and the front light went on. I went to the door and JoAnn greeted me. She was in her Mickey Mouse nightshirt.

"It was just so foggy. I decided I couldn't drive home."

I called Bill.

"What do you mean it's too foggy? There's no fog here. Where are you anyway? You told me you wouldn't be late and it's almost eleven. When are you coming home? Godammit, you and that fuckin' phone company!" He banged the receiver.

"I have to admit that when I heard your car in the driveway I was surprised, but I'm so glad that you decided to come back. I love you, Jackie." JoAnn said as she reached up and put her arms around me and kissed me.

This is what a kiss is supposed to feel like. This is what love feels like.

Chapter 34

Divorce

There was one clear moment in time when I knew Bill and I would divorce, but it evolved slowly and painfully. My job became a career. I was not home every night in time to make dinner. I spent more time on the telephone with people from work. And, of course, there was JoAnn. But, even after JoAnn and I became lovers, I wasn't thinking about divorce. I was living a new and different kind of life.

Bill was feeling lonely and neglected. He called my brother Allan and went to visit him in Boston. He thought he could get some sympathy and maybe some help from Allan. Maybe Allan could talk to me, reason with me, bring me back to my old self. There was no going back. We had all changed and our world was forever different.

Bill started to drink more. He always drank, but only rarely did he drink too much. But he began to drink too much every day. If he went out to dinner with Hank or some other friends, he came home staggering and in a rage.

I imagine that our friends were talking about us, just as I had talked about others in our community who had divorced or had problems that were too grave to keep secret. We socialized with some friends, but less and less frequently. Bill insisted that we have a New Year's Eve party to welcome in 1983. Maybe he thought that getting together with old friends would change the course we were on. Andrew and Anne were both away for the holiday. Andrew was in Gettysburg with his girlfriend and Anne was skiing with friends. Thirty friends or so, came to our house to celebrate.

I've never liked the midnight madness of New Year's Eve. The party hats, the horns, and the noisemakers all seemed like stage props for forced merriment. It was just a reason to drink too much. I always tried to avoid the wet lip-kissing at midnight. Even friends who didn't drink found reason to drink on New Year's Eve. We all drank. The countdown from Times Square was blaring on the TV, Bill poured—mostly spilled—champagne in everyone's glass and, as the ball dropped, I went into the half bath in the downstairs back hall and locked the door.

I could hear the screams of "Happy New Year" and the screech and twists of the noise makers. Over the din I also heard, "Jackie, Jackie, where are you?" Bill said it over and over, getting louder and louder. I was looking at myself in the mirror and talking out loud to the reflection.

"Jackie, Jackie." God, I'm sick of hearing him call me. So what are you going to do, Jack? Go out there and pretend that it's going to be a Happy New Year? Sure, everything is just fine. Fine, fine, fine. Shit, shit, shit. He's right outside the door. Shall I just open it and let him fall in? Can't stay here, Jack. Okay, gotta get out.

The hilarity was dimming and I would have to get coffee and dessert going.

"I'm here, Bill, I'll be right out," I called.

"What are you doing in there anyway?"

"What do you think I'm doing in here?"

I opened the door to his angry face. He grabbed me and gave me a violent kiss. It was wet and open mouthed, and his tongue lashed in and out like a hammer. It hurt. He held me so tightly that it left bruises on my arms.

"Bill, let me go. I have to get the coffee going." I pulled away and worked my way through to the kitchen getting benign hugs and kisses from friends as I went through.

Bill was right behind me.

I managed to get the coffee and dessert out and onto the dining room table. Most people just kept drinking; only a few helped themselves to dessert.

"Great party, Jackie. You guys always have the best parties."

"Next year you'll have to do it again."

"Maybe we should all go somewhere next year, you know, the Bahamas, or Boston."

It must have been 2:30 a.m. before the door closed behind the last guest. Bill was standing in the middle of the living room looking around at the mess. He was a little wobbly.

"Well, that was a good show you put on tonight, running into the bathroom at midnight. How do you think that looked to everyone?" he said.

"What are you talking about? I never have done that midnight thing, you know that. I have to get this place cleaned up a little; I can't face all of it tomorrow."

I began to move around the room and pick up glasses. I passed a few feet from Bill and he grabbed me by the arm and pulled me toward him. I dropped the glasses I was carrying, and they broke on the floor.

"Bill, leave me alone, you're hurting me. My arms already ached from that hug you gave me at midnight." I pushed myself away.

"I'll hurt you all right." He pulled me toward him again, kissing me. He pushed me down on the couch and fell on top of me.

"I'll hurt you all right." I pulled myself out from under him.

"Bill, you're drunk. Cut it out!"

"I'm not drunk and I know what I want. I want you, right now."

"I'm going upstairs and I'm going to sleep in Sarah's room. Now cut it out! What's wrong with you?"

"What's wrong with me? You're asking me what's wrong with me?" he yelled. He walked toward me and gave me a push.

I ran up the stairs went into our bedroom to get some clothes, went into Sarah's room, and shut and locked the door. I could hear him banging around in the kitchen. He slept on the couch in the family room that night. The next day was quiet. We didn't talk about anything.

In 1983, Sarah had progressed at the Institute of Living so that on occasional weekends she could leave the Institute for day visits. I had made plans to pick her up on a Saturday morning in February, drive to New Haven, and take the train to New York City to see a matinee. The theater was Sarah's main interest. JoAnn was making the trip with us, meeting us at the train station. Sarah liked JoAnn. She had gotten to know her from visits we had made to the Institute.

Bill knew about this plan, he had known about it for weeks. But on the Friday night before the trip, he acted like it was new news to him. He had stopped for a drink or two with a friend on his way home from work. He had another martini when he came home. I knew that this plan was nothing he wanted and I had been surprised that he said nothing about it. He didn't like anything I was doing and I knew it. He didn't like my job, he didn't like my friends, he didn't like the time I spent away from the routine of twenty-five years. I knew all of this but I no longer cared what he thought and he knew it. I was feeling a power I had never had before and he was feeling powerless, a brand new feeling for him. I could do whatever I wanted to do.

"I don't like this, I don't like any of this. Why is this JoAnn going with you? Who is she anyway. Call her up and tell her you've changed your mind and you are not going to New York."

"I'm not going to do that. Sarah is all set to go. I am not going to disappoint her. She likes JoAnn and the trip will be good for her."

"Call her up. Call her up right now and call it off."

He picked up the phone and handed it to me. I didn't take it. I moved back, away from him.

"Do it. Do it now, damn it. Who the fuck do you think you are? You and the fuckin' phone company."

He came toward me with his hand raised, waving the receiver.

"Bill, stop! Stop, now."

He pulled the receiver so hard the wire broke off from the base of the phone.

"See what you made me do? You bitch." He raised his hand with the phone; I turned to run and he threw it at me, hard, hitting me in the back. I ran up the stairs.

"Stop, Bill. I'll call the police. Stop."

He stopped in the kitchen and grabbed a knife from the drawer and followed me up the stairs. He stumbled a few times. I ran to the phone in the bedroom and dialed 911.

"Help me, help me. My husband has a knife and he's chasing me. One hundred Carriage Drive. Yes, Weatherwax. Come now!"

I shut the door to the bedroom and pushed a chest up against it. He was on the other side of the door, banging with his fists.

"I'm going to kill myself. I swear I'll do it. It's either you or me. I'm going to kill one of us tonight. I can't take this shit anymore."

"I've called 911 and the cops will be here any minute. Back away and put the knife down."

"You called the cops? Why? Oh, God, why?"

Just then the doorbell rang. I looked out the window and saw the police cruiser in front of the house with its lights flashing.

Bill put the knife under the couch and answered the door.

"Everything is fine here officer, really," he said.

"Where is your wife? We'd like to see her," the officer said.

"She's fine. She's upstairs."

"We won't leave until we see her and talk to her."

"Jackie, come down here for a minute," Bill called.

I heard the voices. I pushed the chest away from the door and went to the top of the stairs.

"I'm here, officer," I said in a quiet but shaky voice.

"Mrs. Weatherwax, are you all right? Can we talk to you for a minute?"

I could see Bill out of the corner of my eye. He was sitting down with his hands on his head curled over.

I walked down the stairs and stood with the police in the front hall.

"I'm okay, officer. I was afraid, and that's why I called. We had an argument, but it's over now."

"Are you sure you're all right and that we don't need to take any action here?"

"Yes, officer, we're okay now."

"Mr. Weatherwax, is everything under control here?"

"Yes, officer, everything is under control." Bill stood up and the police left.

Bill went back to the living room and put his head down in his hands again. I went upstairs and went to bed in Sarah's room with a chest pushed up against the locked door. I didn't sleep. It was over.

Chapter 35

Moving Out

Two weeks after that violent February evening, I filed for divorce and had the papers served to Bill. I was counseled by my attorney to stay living in the house. It is sort of like squatter's rights; if you are there with your things, no one can take them away from you. Sounds like it makes sense, but it was impossible to do safely. I stayed until the end of May and moved out to my own small apartment in New Haven.

I loved that apartment. It was all mine. I was alone in it and could do whatever I wanted. I had never felt so liberated. As a matter of fact, I had never, ever been alone before. I took only a few things from the house in Glastonbury. Bill and I met one day and went over what I could and could not take. This was all prior to the divorce. I could take a couch and a chair. I was allowed the kitchen table and three of the six chairs that went with it. I bought new dishes and flatware. The chairs were a problem when Andrew, Anne, and Sarah came to visit at the same time. Andrew would have to borrow a chair from Bill and return it after dinner. We laughed about it, but it wasn't funny.

It didn't surprise any of the kids that we were separated and were headed for divorce. I had driven to Providence to tell Anne about what was happening.

"It's a relief, Mom," Anne said. "There's been such tension in the house for so long. I'm glad it's over. I've talked to Andrew about it and he feels the same way I do. It hasn't been easy being around you and dad."

We spent the afternoon walking around the RISD campus. We had dinner together. Anne would be graduating in June and was undecided about what to do. She thought she would stay in Providence and work as a bartender for the summer. She liked the city and had good friends who would be there for the summer, too.

Andrew had left Gettysburg College midway through his junior year and was at the Hart School of Music at the University of Hartford. He loved what he was doing. He was an outstanding trumpet player and a creative composer of jazz. He didn't love being home alone with Bill. Bill was drinking too much all the time and Andrew was there to see it and live through it. He loved me and knew the divorce was inevitable, but he resented me for having left him alone with his father. He is a gentle soul and could never bring himself to rage against me, but I knew how he felt. It would take time and his moving out of the house for our relationship to soften.

I had spoken to Sarah's doctor, Dr. Boynton, about our marital problems and then about our divorce. Sarah knew that life on Carriage Drive was not smooth.

"Sarah is not that fragile. She is much stronger than you think." Dr. Boynton reassured me.

There was only one way to talk to Sarah and that was to be honest and direct with her. There would be no pretending, no coloring the truth, no insincerity, just straight honest talk. And, of course, to listen to her, hear her, and love her.

Sarah was finishing high school at the Institute and would be discharged and attend Hartford College for Women in September, 1984. Dr. Boynton thought that starting out at Hartford College was best since it was close to the Institute if she should need support during her transition out of the hospital. I had worried about Sarah rejoining the Glastonbury community. What would that be like for her? How would she explain where she had been? What would she say to her friends from years ago? She never had to do that. She transferred after one year at Hartford College for Women to Emerson College in Boston.

The divorce went on and on and on. Bill was enraged and determined that if I as going to leave, I would leave with nothing. He fought me at every turn. We had court appearances about things like which Christmas tree decorations were mine and which decorations were his. We had a Ford Fiesta and an Audi sedan. I was driving the sedan and he had the state police stop me, claiming I had stolen the car. Both cars were in Bill's name. Documents such as checking accounts, savings accounts, wills, and letters had to be filed with the court. Depositions took place. What kind of mother had I been? How did I care for the house? Did I neglect my responsibilities in any way?

My sales manager from work had to appear in court and answer questions about me and my performance at work. How much money did I make? How much money could I make? Who did I have lunch with every day? JoAnn's name was never mentioned during the trial or deposition. I never knew why. I guessed that maybe Bill would have been even more humiliated if my relationship with JoAnn became a factor in the divorce.

The judge, after a year of battle, declared that I should get one half of all assets. In other words, I had been a good wife and mother for twenty-five years and deserved half of whatever there was, including Bill's pension and 401k. Bill went wild.

"That money is mine and only mine. I've worked my ass off for that and you're not going to get one cent. You want out of this? You get out, but not with my money."

He had his lawyer file an appeal.

"Oh God, I can't take this. I can't do this anymore." I was as wild as Bill, but I was worn down.

Bill's lawyer was a tough guy. He was a fierce fighter. His wife had left him the year before and he hated all women. I could see it in his eyes when he questioned me. He was seeing his own wife, not me.

I changed lawyers. I don't know why, except that I needed to take action, any action. I felt trapped. The judge that handed down the fifty-fifty split of assets died quite suddenly. My sense of desperation increased even though I knew that judge would have nothing to do with the appeal. The case would go to another court.

My mother called after Bill filed the appeal.

"Jackie, why don't you just stick it out? You've been together for twenty-five years. Can't you just stay with him?"

"What are you saying?" I yelled into the phone. "Do you hear what you're asking me? Don't you care about me at all?"

"Well, it's costing so much money and what will people say? What will they think?"

"I don't care what anybody thinks. You're asking me to throw away the rest of my life. You don't care about me. You care more about what people will think about *you*."

"Now, Jackie, don't get so excited. This isn't like you."

"Yes, Mom, this is exactly like me. You don't know me. That's the problem."

"Well, you know there's a family reunion next month. You got the invitation from Jean, didn't you? She's having the reunion at her lake house." She wouldn't stop.

"Yes, I got it."

"Well, when you go, if anyone asks you about Bill, just tell them he's away on a business trip."

"No, Mom, I won't. And if that's what you want, I just won't go. I'm not going to pretend that everything is fine when nothing is fine. I'm not ashamed or embarrassed by getting a divorce. You are."

"I don't know why you're getting so excited. Of course I want you to go. I just didn't want to have to explain everything to the whole family. You know how they are."

"I know how you are, Mom. I think it would be better if I didn't go, so then you can say whatever you want to everyone there. Just tell them all that we're both away on business trips!"

My mother never brought up the subject of divorce again. I didn't go to the reunion. The conversation with my mother gave me a good reason not to go. The truth is, I certainly didn't want to spend the day talking about Bill and the reasons for the divorce.

I liked my new lawyer about as much as I liked the old one. That is, I didn't like her at all. The difference was a new voice to listen to and a new face to look at. The clock still ran every time I called or had any contact with her. My new lawyer told me all the things my old lawyer should have and didn't. I was sick of the whole thing. I made two attempts to talk to Bill alone about the divorce.

"We're giving all this money to the lawyers. Can't we settle this ourselves?" I pleaded with him.

"As long as you want my 401k and pension money, no we can't settle it."

"But think of what it's costing."

"Hey, you wanted this thing, not me. You back away from that money and I'll talk to you."

I felt stuck like glue to him and the divorce. He had a way about him that stopped the world around him. There was never a way to push Bill to do anything he didn't want to do. He slowed down and made you wait with him. Even when we were separated he kept sticky ties to me.

"Where have you been? I've been trying to reach you for days," he'd say when he called on the phone.

"What do you mean 'you've been trying to reach me for days'? What do you want?"

"I want to know where you've been."

"You're not my boss, Bill. Remember, we're not married anymore and I don't have to answer to you about where I am or what I do." I loved saying that.

"You're such a smartass."

The appeal was snarled in the court system for about six months, and I decided I couldn't take it anymore. I knew that it was just what they wanted. I could almost hear Bill's lawyer saying, "Don't worry, she'll get tired of this whole thing and you'll get just what you want."

I called my lawyer and told her that I just wanted to settle and get it done. The whole thing was consuming my energy for everything else. I wanted to get through with it, to move away from it, and get unstuck from him. He had a power over me; every time I saw him I felt pulled in to the old role I had with him. I hated that and hated me with him.

Chapter 36

Breaking Open

It felt like being shot from a gun. The surge of energy was huge. That was certainly part of the change I was experiencing, but it was much more than that. The "Little Woman" was gone. I left her there with Bill on Carriage Drive in Glastonbury. My career at SNET was on the move. There was a column titled, "Promotions & Moves & Changes" in the company newspaper that was published each week. Over the next ten years, I moved from sales to managing a 250-person department, then on to running a startup business for the company and, finally, I became a director.

I was totally energized by work. I loved sales and found I had a real talent for it. It required keen listening skills, insight, and perception about people—all qualities that I had. The years of therapy probably helped. I was selling complex telecommunication systems to big businesses all over Connecticut. I drove through every nook and cranny of the state, not because I had customers in every corner but because I was lost most of the time.

We had sales meetings every Monday morning at 8:00 a.m. I was the only woman in our sales group. I liked the camaraderie we shared. It was silly stuff, but it worked and made me feel like I belonged. I had a good working relationship with everyone in the group. The bottom line was that I was doing a very good job bringing in sales and that was what it was all about. The group had great respect for the bottom line and great respect for the commissions good sales garnered. Most of the group stayed in the office on Mondays to clean up paperwork and have lunch together. It was good to share stories about what was going on in the company and with customers. Sales is a lonely job, so it took some work to stay connected.

Bill had the state police stop me because he said I stole his car, the Audi. They didn't arrest me or demand that I relinquish the car there on Route 91, but I was served with a piece of paper that explained that the car was in Bill's name and that I should return it to him. It also said that he would let me use the other car, a nifty Ford Fiesta. We arranged a meeting and exchanged cars, a nice even swap.

I never thought about whose name was on our mutual property. Both cars were in Bill's name. The whole car buying process was such a huge project for him that I could understand why they were always in his name. It took about a year for him to make a deal. Saturday after Saturday we trudged around to various dealers—just looking at cars. About ten years into the marriage I wised up and when it was car purchase time and the question came up about looking, I changed my response.

"When you are ready to buy, let me know and I'll go with you to see the car but I'm not going with you to look anymore."

"But how do you know what you want unless you look first?"

He made charts and graphs and studied everything there was to know about all the cars. He knew what he wanted. I think he liked looking and deciding. I didn't. You need a car; you buy a car; that was my approach.

The Ford Fiesta sometimes started and sometimes didn't. I had to get a dependable car. I knew that I wanted a Toyota Camry, a dark red and beige two-tone with beige leather seats. I went to the nearest Toyota dealership in New Haven. The showroom was busy with people browsing and a few serious buyers sitting at desks with salesmen. It was Saturday, so I was dressed casually in jeans and a sweater. I strolled around the showroom looking at the models on display and checking the list prices. I picked up a brochure that featured the very car I wanted, a real beauty. No one approached me. There was a free salesman standing at the window looking out at the sea of cars in the parking lot.

"Excuse me, can you help me?"

He turned and looked at me.

"Did you want something?" he asked.

"Yes, I'd like to buy a car." He looked at me again and then looked around me and behind me.

"Is your husband here?"

"No, he isn't."

"You're just looking. Go right ahead. Let me know if you have any questions." He turned to resume his stare out the window.

I'm a woman, I can't buy a car without a man. Son of a bitch.

"Excuse me again, are you a salesman here?"

"Yes, I am."

"Well, I said I wanted to buy a car today. Are you sure you are a salesman here? Do you want to sell me a car?"

"Are you sure you want to buy a car and not just look at the cars?"

"May I please see the manager? Where is he? Just tell me where he is so you don't have to stop looking out the window." Yes, I was angry.

He pointed to an office at the back of the showroom with a large glass window and the blinds drawn shut. The sign on the door read, "Mr. John Manzi, Manager." I knocked on the door and heard, "Yeah, okay, wait a second." I was in a mini rage and "wait a second" was not going to work. I knocked again. I heard, "Yeah, yeah, wait a second." By now, Mr. Salesman was behind me waiting with me.

"Come in, come in."

I opened the door and went into the office. The desk was covered with papers. There as a bookcase behind the desk filled with brochures scattered in no particular order. Mr. Manzi was in a wrinkled suit that was a least a size too big for him. There was a strong smell of cheap aftershave lotion, more like a cover up for bad body odor.

"Joe, what's going on here?" Manzi looked at Joe, not me.

"Damned if I know. She said she wanted to look at the showroom cars, and I said 'Sure go right ahead.'"

"That's not what I said at all. I said I wanted to buy a car today. Do you want to sell car today?" Manzi was still looking at Joe Salesman.

"Excuse me, Mr. Manzi, I'm talking to you."

Manzi looked at me quickly and turned away.

"Joe, take care of this girl, will you please?"

Girl! What's with these "boys?" What are they afraid of? Can't make eye contact with a woman? I wouldn't buy a car from these guys if it meant driving that fucking Ford Fiesta for the next five years.

"No, Joe, don't bother to 'take care of this girl.' I wouldn't buy a car from you boys if you were the last dealership in America. By the way, I'll be telling everyone I know that this is definitely not the place to buy anything. As a matter of fact, I will be telling everyone in the showroom as I leave." I turned to leave the boys.

"Wait just a minute, miss." Manzi came to life. "I'll help you personally. Let me show you around."

"Too late. I'm on my way to A-1 Toyota in North Haven."

By this time I was in the middle of the showroom. I was speaking in a very loud voice and had the full attention of everyone around the room.

"I'm on my way to A-1 Toyota," I yelled again as I exited the front door. I heard Manzi mutter "bitch" behind me. I turned, smiled, and waved. I went to A-1 Toyota and I bought my red and beige Toyota. I closed the deal quickly and easily. Once I knew the price of the car, I sat with the salesman and pulled out my checkbook.

I said, "I want that car, this is what I want to pay for it, and I am ready right now to give you a deposit."

He did the usual back and forth with the "big manager man." It was such a show. We went back and forth twice, but I held my ground and got the car I wanted at the price I wanted to pay. It took about forty-five minutes. I could pick the car up the following Tuesday.

We shook hands and the deal was done. Did I like the salesmen there any better than in New Haven? No, but at least he looked me in the eye, and at least he knew I was a customer.

Did I feel good? Oh, yes I did. I should have taped the whole thing for Bill.

Chapter 37

Coming Out

Being closeted about one's sexuality is not easy, but coming out is not easy either. Let me start with my own acceptance about my new sexual identity. First, there was the phase "I'm not a lesbian. I just love JoAnn." It made sense to me. How could I be a lesbian? I was married and had three children, as if that was proof forever that I was not a lesbian. It was, however, a shield for as long as I wanted to stay behind it.

Like all other change, it took time to accept. This was my own private tug of war. It didn't need resolution, really, because I didn't need a label. But the push and pull of it stayed in a quiet corner of my mind. With so much unsettled, "I'm not a lesbian, I just love JoAnn" was fine for a while.

I lived a double life for a whole year. Several times during that year when the pressure grew to an intolerable level, I made attempts at breaking the tie with JoAnn. I tried to stop seeing her. I tried to stop talking to her. I couldn't do it. My life was empty without her.

For a very long time I didn't let myself think about telling my kids about JoAnn. While I was still living at home there was no need to say anything. They all knew that Bill and I were having problems or, more accurately, more problems than usual. Even after I had moved out of the house into my own apartment there was no need to say anything. It was only after the divorce was final and JoAnn and I bought a house together that I had to face the realities with them.

Deep down, I think they all knew that my relationship with JoAnn was more than house sharing. But, it is one thing for them to think something and quite another for me to tell them. I told myself, *If they ask the question, they have to be willing to hear the answer.* I was hoping that they would ask the question. Anne asked and she knew the answer.

It was a dark and rainy Saturday. I was in the basement doing laundry. It was mid afternoon and my phone rang. I had an old, black wall phone right near the washing machine.

"Hi, Mom," Anne said.

"Hi, Anne, how are you?" Anne had graduated from Rhode Island School of Design the year before but decided to stay in Providence for a while. She was a bartender at a popular waterfront bar.

"I'm okay. How are you?"

"I'm fine. Busy at work. But I love it." I stopped putting the clothes in the dryer and was looking around at the 150-year-old basement that I loved.

"How's JoAnn?"

"She's fine." I stopped looking around.

"I want to ask you something about her. Do you mind?"

"No, of course not." I was staring at the big, black soapstone double sink. *Here it comes. I feel it.*

"Your relationship with her is more than just friends, isn't it?" I kept staring at the sink. I spoke but I could not hear my own voice.

"Yes, Anne, it is," I answered.

"I thought so. I'm glad I asked. I like her."

"Thanks." I still could not hear my voice.

"I love you, Mom."

"I love you, too."

We said goodbye and hung up. I stayed in the basement for I don't know how long. When I awakened from my dazed state, I went upstairs and told JoAnn. We celebrated quietly.

"She may tell Andrew and Sarah," JoAnn said.

"Yes, but I'll still have to talk to them. I'm wiped out from just this call."

"Come on now, Jackie, this is good news today. Let's enjoy it. You're still their mother and they will always love you."

I didn't always believe that they would love me. The guilt I carried got in the way. Andrew struggled with his relationship with me. He felt abandoned by me, left alone with his father. I was sure he blamed JoAnn. Even after he left the house and had his own apartment, Bill called on him all the time for any reason or sometimes no reason at all. When Bill drank too much, Andrew was the first one he called. We met for dinner often.

"Mom, can we meet alone without JoAnn."

Andrew said it every time we made a plan. He didn't have to, because I knew he wanted to meet with me only. I took comfort in the fact that we never stopped talking. I have always felt that he and I were most alike. I tried hard to relax when I was with him. I never quite did, but I always felt his love.

Everything changed when Andrew met his future wife, Josafina. I was sure that Josa knew that JoAnn and I were partners and it would be like her to say something like 'What's the big deal? Your mom is happy." Although it took months for us to talk about it, Andrew was more relaxed with me and JoAnn. Slowly, JoAnn was included in our dinners together.

In some ways, Sarah knew JoAnn better than Andrew or Anne. We had visited Sarah at the Institute of Living many times. They related to each other without the complications of the outside world. She had no preconceived ideas about us, no assumptions. She loved me and she loved JoAnn from the first time she met her. Sarah had been disconnected from the family for over four years. It gave her an objectivity that the others didn't have.

This was the beginning. The guilt I felt never wholly went away. For many years when the phone rang and one of them asked me for something, anything, I would feel like I had to say yes—not just yes, but "Yes, of course, whatever you want." I couldn't say no to any of them. Did I have the right to say no? It was a hard lesson to learn. There is no one point in time when we change. It was slow and sometimes painful. I was happy, so how could that be a bad thing? But nothing is ever one thing or another. I was very happy in my new life with JoAnn, but somehow, underneath the happiness was the nagging sense that I had no right to be happy. We make mistakes and then have to go on and on paying for them. We learn to live with ambivalence, with the gray joy that has a tinge of sadness in it.

Telling other family members and friends was no less difficult, but had much less heat and no guilt attached to it. I gradually stopped thinking about life as a big popularity contest. None of us can win that one. As my confidence increased, so did my ability to let go of the need to be popular. I still protected myself, however. I was never going to tell my mother. I know she thought about me and wondered about my sexuality, but she never asked because she never wanted to know the answer. She always loved me, but I feel certain that she was disappointed in me, too.

If I had let myself think about my brother and sister first, I would have known what to expect. I knew them well. I knew that my brother Bill would embrace me no matter what I told him. I knew my brother Allan would not. My sister was like my mother; she would love me, but be surprised and disappointed. I felt a whole lot of angst that I didn't need to feel. I can now report it in a breezy way. It was not breezy in the doing.

Friends were a different matter. I found out that most of them were not friends at all, so that eliminated a whole big group. Other people didn't care one way or another. At most, it made for an interesting story to tell over coffee, especially in suburbia where there isn't much interesting going on anyway. Those who dropped us when they found out that Sarah had a mental illness were also the ones that held their hands up in horror at my switch in sexual preference.

Then there were my dear friends, just a few, that waited patiently for me to tell them about my new life. I couldn't be a close friend without sharing such a big part of my life. For a time, I couldn't tell anyone. This meant that my relationship with these precious few was lopsided, on hold, stilted, and without substance for a while.

"We've been waiting for you to say something. For God's sake, what did you think would happen if you told us.?"

"We knew what was going on; we're not stupid."

"I gave you every opening I could think of."

"We love you, Jack. We want you to be happy."

"What's the big fuckin' deal anyway?"

The passage of time shrinks some things. But ask me if I would go back and do it all again? The answer is that I am glad to be where I am now.

Chapter 38

Christmas Cheer

What was to have been a simple matter, turned into a dark hole where even Christmas decorations were reason for hot debate. But it was finally over, finished, ended. We could go our own separate ways.

But like so many things, the end of one big thing is the beginning of another even bigger thing. Life had to have a new order and routine. What about birthdays, graduations, parents' weekends? What about holidays? What about Thanksgiving and Christmas? Christmas was the big one. We decided we'd be fair by agreeing to alternate; one year I'd have Christmas Eve and Bill would have Christmas Day and then we'd switch. That was fair and fine. But what would I do when it wasn't my turn on Christmas Eve or Christmas Day?

"You'll come with me to my brother's house," JoAnn said.

That's not how it was supposed to be. We were supposed to spend those holidays with our own family, not someone else's. I didn't know if I could do it. How would I feel? Wouldn't I be better off just staying home alone? I didn't even know JoAnn's family. I had only met them once or twice. Wouldn't they think it was strange that I didn't have my own family to celebrate with?

"You'll be fine. You'll be with me. They're nice people," JoAnn said. *I'm sure they're nice people. They'll be welcoming and friendly. That's not the big thing. The big thing is how will I feel? How will I feel about what they might be thinking about me?*

"Who is she?"

"Does she have a family?"

"Why isn't she with her own family?"

"Don't they care about her?"

Yes, that's what I was thinking, "Who am I, anyway?" It was the whole Christmas thing and how we should all be with our family, but it was also the issue of Jackie and JoAnn being together. Which one of those made me feel worse? It was a toss up, but the family Christmas connection was the toughest one for me in those first years after the divorce.

I bought something nice for Jim and Jen, JoAnn's brother and sister-in—law. I can't remember what it was but JoAnn was certain they would appreciate it. I also brought a bottle of scotch hoping that Jim would offer some to me. JoAnn never said she had any apprehension about the day, but I knew she did. I sensed a small, growing tension as we got ready to drive to West Haven for the day.

JoAnn's family was small, consisting of Jim and Jen, their two children, and her mother, and father. Jen had other family who came to celebrate the holiday.

The house was full when we arrived. That was probably the good news. *Maybe I can find a seat somewhere and just sit and smile for the day. Is JoAnn just going to ignore me and leave me to sit and smile alone?*

"Jackie come here I want you to meet the Germes. (Jen's sister's family)" *I wish she would just leave me alone to sit and smile.*

"You remember my father don't you?"

"Yes, of course I do. Nice to see you again."

"And this is Jen's mom, Ann Currie, and that's Jen's dad, Alan, over there alone next to the fireplace." I waved to him, but he didn't wave back. He looked like he enjoyed sitting alone.

"Do you want a drink?"

"Of course I want a drink."

"Come with me to the kitchen and I'll get you one."

No one else drinks here? Another thing for me to feel weird about. Jim has a drink and Alan has a drink and now I have a drink. Does Jim's brother-in-law have one? No. What about the other women? No, not a one. Just me. Too bad. I'm not taking that one on. I've got enough to worry about without the drink thing. Sit and take a sip. Let the scotch work. Relax. Don't try to make conversation. Nobody cares. They're all too busy with each other and opening gifts. And don't make eye contact with anyone. You'll only have to say something. Better off quiet without words. Just watch and listen.

The gifts were flying, and paper and ribbon were all over the floor. Samantha, Jim and Jen's daughter, was opening lots of gifts from her Aunt

JoAnn. Great red rubber boots with Donald Duck on the front, perfect with the red slicker and yellow umbrella. Sam loved them, tried them on right away, and said she would wear them to kindergarten on the first day back after vacation. Sam opened another gift, something that came in a small box. It looked like a jewelry box.

"What's this?" Sam asked.

She held up a thin, small silver chain with a very small white bead on it.

No one seemed to know what it was. It didn't look like anything I had ever seen before. Then Ann Currie looked up.

"Sam, that's an add-a-pearl necklace from me and gramps. Isn't it beautiful?"

Sam didn't answer. She put it back in the box.

"Sammy, every year for your birthday and for Christmas I'll buy you another pearl and before you know it you'll have a nice long necklace. Isn't that wonderful?"

"Do you want another drink, Jackie?" Jim asked.

"Yes, thanks."

"Jackie, are you sure you want another drink? We'll be eating soon," JoAnn whispered.

"Yes, I'm sure. Very sure," I whispered back.

"Where's your family today?" Chris Germe asked.

"They're with their father today. They were with me last night."

There, I said it. And I said it with a smile. Did you all hear me? I'm not with my kids because this year he has them on Christmas Day. Next year I won't be here with you I'll be with them. It will be my turn to have Christmas.

Stop, stop right now. Be nice, it's not their fault that you are here like some displaced person.

I hate it, I really hate it here. I don't care how nice they are, I don't want to be here. I don't want to be anyplace right now. Where the fuck is JoAnn? There she is trying to make small talk with Mr. Currie. He seems to speak only in yes's and no's. Look at that. He's getting up to go.

"Ann, I'm leaving are you coming with me?"

"Alan, we haven't had dinner yet."

"I know we haven't had dinner, I'm going home are you coming with me or not?"

I was surprised how quickly the dinner was over given how much food there was on the table. There was an Italian antipasto, and then Italian manicotti, both made by JoAnn's mother and father. After that, they served a pork roast with all the trimmings. Jen's sisters each brought their special casseroles. I don't remember what I ate. I just remember feeling physically very uncomfortable. I couldn't wait for dessert, not because I wanted any, but because it signaled the end of the meal.

At last the day was over. Ann packed a big dinner to take home for Alan. JoAnn tried to help Jen clear the table.

"Thanks, but don't bother with that now. Jim and I will take care of it," she said.

"Sammy, here's your add-a-pearl necklace near the crumpled up Christmas paper. Be careful not to lose it or throw it away by mistake."

The crowd gathered up their gifts and empty casserole and serving dishes. I went upstairs to get our coats.

"So nice to meet you, Jackie," Chris Germe said. "Maybe we'll see you next year."

I ached inside, but I smiled and said thank you and good-bye.

Me and JoAnn

JoAnn and Me

Me and JoAnn

Sarah, Anne, Josa, Andrew

Sarah, Anne, me, Andrew Josafina and baby Tyler

Anne, Me, Andrew, Bill, Sarah

Sarah (age 4)

Sarah

Andrew and Anne

Me and Anne

Sarah (age 13)

Chapter 39

Today

Today our Christmases are full of joy and happiness. We share Christmas with both of our families. The arc of almost thirty years has brought us to a place of deep emotional intimacy, a place I never thought I could find. JoAnn knows me and loves me. I know her and love her. It validates who we are when we are loved in that way. I am full of wonder that I have found this life with her.

Sarah is now an actor and voice coach. Anne is a sculptor and painter. Andrew is a web marketing strategy expert. They all write . . . short stories, novels, poetry, and music. They are what they do. They found their passions and pursued them. They are true to themselves.

As it will, life has made changes for us all. Tyler, Elias, and Miles—three grandsons—are with us. Tyler is seven years old and met his parents, Josa and Andrew, a few days after he was born. Elias is six years old and Miles is eighteen months old. They belong to Sarah and Eileen in Toronto. They are innocent as only new life can be and here to remind us that life continues, fresh and full of hope and the wonder of what can be. This love is beautiful, pure, and uncomplicated. Anne and her partner, Joyce, are loving aunties. This beautiful family has enriched JoAnn's and my life immensely.

Our life in Boston is full with many friends. JoAnn has had a rewarding career as a senior executive and consultant and most recently, was appointed CEO of a software startup. She has also dedicated herself to advancing women into positions of leadership and influence through her work with The Boston Club. She is a frequent speaker and advisor on these topics.

The challenges don't go away, but there is a balance now with love and joy. Andrew has been a man of strong conviction to do only what he loved to do. He spent years exploring music, woodworking, and building. Financially it was a challenge. He then found he had a passion for web marketing and did it well. He started a business with two friends that grew and caught the attention of a very large and successful company which was eager to acquire their expertise. How provident that was. Andrew was diagnosed with Parkinson's disease in 2003. He and his partners sold their company. Andrew could retire and be financially comfortable. He has become a Buddhist and we, too, are all working hard to "live in the moment."

Where am I today? What have I learned from this journey? What do I know? What don't I know? I know that I grew and thrived in a successful career that took me from sales to business development to running a broadband company and loving it. I know that I continue to grow and learn and pursue my interests and passions. I know that JoAnn is the love of my life. I know there is not just one way to live this life; there are many ways. I know that pain and suffering are every bit as much a part of life as joy and pleasure. I know that every question can have many answers. I know that love is key. I know too, that it hurts. And I know that life is rich and wondrous.

Like most people, I've been through many twists and turns in my life. I've had challenges and obstacles to overcome and crises to endure. It hasn't been an easy journey. Today, I know who I am, I like who I am, and I am comfortable in my own shoes. I wish this for all who read my book.

Epilogue

This book has been resting on a shelf for several years. I was unsure of the wisdom of sharing my story. I made several attempts to publish this book, but what I heard was, "There is no money in your story," or "This is not compelling, unusual, or different." Perhaps, but for me, the writing has allowed me to look at my life up close again to examine it, explore it, and feel it again. It has been a private and sometimes painful therapy. I hope the reading of my story has been an interesting journey for you and that it has provided some insight, inspiration, joy, and hope.

"To exist is to change; to change is to mature; to mature is to go on creating oneself endlessly."

—Henri Bergson